TOKYO TR
GUIDE 2023

"Tokyo Unveiled: A Comprehensive Travel Guide to Japan's Dynamic Capital. "Discover the Hidden Gems, Cultural Delights, and Vibrant Cityscape of Tokyo"

By

Esther .L George

Table of Contents

Preface	6
Introduction;Essential Tokyo	7
History of Tokyo	11
Expense of travel	19
Entry criteria and visas	26
List of international flying companies	37
Tips for success; What first-time visitors to Japan should do and not do is listed below:	37
Travel insurance	42
Telecommunication	46
The Airalo app	49
Activities for family	51
Facts about Tokyo	54
7days itenary	57
Festivals and events	61
Packing list	65
Rules for taking photos	68
Transportation in Tokyo	72
The Suica card	79

Car rental companies	82
Accommodation Options	85
Booking advice and popular lodging choices	92
Accommodation & prices	95
Dining in Tokyo	99
Popular eateries, rates and restaurants	105
Choices for vegetarians and vegans	112
Exploring Shinjuku	115
Discovering Shibuya	122
Unveiling Asakusa	130
Ueno Park and Museums	137
Odaiba: Tokyo's Futuristic Island	144
Exploring Old Tokyo: Yanaka and Nezu	148
Tokyo's Temples and Shrines	156
Gardens and Parks in Tokyo	163
Tokyo by Night	170
Tokyo hidden gem	173
Things I found interest on my visit to Tokyo	177
FAQs	178

Advice on How to Save Money in Tokyo 180

Conclusion: Tokyo Unveiled 182

Copyright © 2023 by Esther L.George
All rights reserved.

No part of this book may be reproduced, stored in a retrieval system, or transmitted, in any form or by any means, electronic, mechanical, photocopying, recording, or otherwise, without the prior written

permission of the publisher or author, except in the case of brief

quotations embodied in critical reviews and certain other non- commercial uses permitted by copyright.

Preface

As you hold this travel guide in your hands, prepare to embark on an unforgettable journey through the heart of Japan's dynamic capital. Tokyo Unveiled is not just a mere compilation of tourist attractions; it is a gateway to discovering the hidden gems, cultural nuances, and the soul of this remarkable city.

In this comprehensive travel guide, we will delve deep into the multifaceted layers of Tokyo, from its rich history and awe-inspiring architecture to its cutting-edge technology and gastronomic delights. Whether you are a first-time visitor or a seasoned traveler, this book will serve as your trusted companion, offering valuable insights and expert recommendations to make the most of your time in this captivating city.

We would appreciate you leaving a review of this book on Amazon to help us improve

Safe Travels

Esther L. George

Introduction;Essential Tokyo

we will delve into the essential aspects of Tokyo, providing you with valuable information to make your visit to this vibrant city an unforgettable experience. From must-see attractions to local customs, let's explore the essence of Tokyo.

Tokyo's Iconic Landmarks:
Tokyo is brimming with iconic landmarks that showcase its unique blend of tradition and modernity. Here are some must-visit places:

a. Tokyo Skytree: Standing at a towering height of 634 meters, the Tokyo Skytree offers breathtaking panoramic views of the city. Take the elevator to the observation decks and enjoy the magnificent vista.

b. Senso-ji Temple: Located in Asakusa, Senso-ji Temple is Tokyo's oldest and most famous Buddhist temple. Marvel at the grand entrance gate (Kaminarimon) and immerse yourself in the vibrant atmosphere of Nakamise Shopping Street leading to the temple.

c. Meiji Shrine: Nestled in the heart of bustling Shibuya, Meiji Shrine is a tranquil oasis dedicated to Emperor Meiji and Empress Shoken. Take a serene stroll through the expansive grounds and experience the tranquility of this spiritual haven.

d. Imperial Palace: Explore the Imperial Palace in Chiyoda, the primary residence of the Emperor of Japan. While the inner grounds are only open on special occasions, the picturesque gardens surrounding the palace offer a glimpse of its regal beauty.

Tokyo's Neighborhoods:
Tokyo is a city of diverse neighborhoods, each with its own distinctive character and attractions. Here are a few noteworthy areas to explore:

a. Shibuya: Known for its iconic scramble crossing and vibrant nightlife, Shibuya is a hub of fashion, shopping, and entertainment. Visit the famous Hachiko Statue and indulge in shopping at Shibuya 109.

b. Shinjuku: Boasting the busiest train station in the world, Shinjuku is a bustling district with towering skyscrapers, neon lights, and a vibrant nightlife scene. Explore the Kabukicho entertainment district and enjoy panoramic views from the observation decks of the Tokyo Metropolitan Government Building.

c. Harajuku: A fashion and youth culture mecca, Harajuku offers a unique blend of avant-garde fashion, quirky street art, and trendy shops. Takeshita Street is a must-visit, known for its vibrant fashion boutiques and street food stalls.

d. Akihabara: Delve into the world of anime, manga, and electronics in Akihabara. This district is a haven for tech enthusiasts and pop culture aficionados, with numerous shops selling gadgets, manga, and anime merchandise.

Experiencing Tokyo's Cuisine and Nightlife:
Tokyo is a culinary paradise, offering a wide range of traditional and international cuisines. Sample authentic sushi, savor a bowl of ramen, or indulge in mouthwatering street food at bustling food markets such as Tsukiji Fish Market and Ameya-Yokocho Market. Don't forget to try the vibrant nightlife of Tokyo, with its countless bars, clubs, and izakayas (Japanese-style pubs) in areas like Roppongi and Ginza.

Navigating Tokyo's Transportation:
Tokyo's public transportation system is known for its efficiency and convenience. Utilize the extensive network of trains, subways, and buses to navigate the city easily. Consider purchasing a prepaid IC card like Suica or Pasmo for seamless travel across different modes of transportation.

Etiquette and Customs:
Respect for Japanese customs and etiquette will greatly enhance your experience in Tokyo. Remember to bow when greeting.

History of Tokyo

Once a humble fishing village known as Edo, Tokyo has transformed into a thriving metropolis that pulsates with innovation, culture, and a rich history. Here is a unique and concise overview of Tokyo's captivating past:

1. Edo Period (1603-1868): Tokyo's story begins during the Edo period when it served as the seat of power for the Tokugawa shogunate. Under strict isolationist policies, Edo grew into a bustling city, its economy flourishing with commerce and trade. The samurai class held influence, and traditional arts such as kabuki theater and ukiyo-e prints thrived.

2. Meiji Restoration (1868): The Meiji Restoration marked a turning point for Tokyo. With the emperor's return to power, Edo was renamed Tokyo, meaning "Eastern Capital." The nation embarked on a rapid modernization process, embracing Western ideas, technology, and infrastructure. The city's landscape underwent significant transformations, with the construction of railway systems, Western-style buildings, and the Imperial Palace.

3. Great Kanto Earthquake (1923): Tokyo faced a devastating earthquake in 1923, known as the Great Kanto Earthquake. The disaster caused widespread destruction, fires, and loss of life. Despite the immense challenges, Tokyo displayed its resilience by rebuilding the city rapidly, incorporating modern urban planning principles and innovative architectural designs.

4. World War II and Post-War Reconstruction: Tokyo suffered severe damage during World War II due to extensive bombings. The post-war era

witnessed a remarkable recovery as Tokyo rebuilt itself once again. The city emerged as a symbol of Japan's economic resurgence, experiencing rapid growth and development.

5. 1964 Olympics and Economic Boom: Tokyo hosted the 1964 Summer Olympics, which became a significant milestone in Japan's recovery and international recognition. The event showcased Tokyo's technological advancements and efficiency. Following the Olympics, the city experienced a remarkable economic boom, establishing itself as a global financial and technological hub.

6. Contemporary Tokyo: Present-day Tokyo continues to captivate visitors with its vibrant blend of tradition and innovation. The city stands at the forefront of technology, fashion, and pop culture. Iconic landmarks like the Tokyo Skytree and Shibuya Crossing have become symbols of its modern identity. Tokyo also prides itself on preserving its historical sites, such as Asakusa's Senso-ji Temple and the

Imperial Palace, allowing visitors to glimpse into its storied past.

This brief journey through Tokyo's history showcases its ability to adapt, reinvent, and embrace change while preserving its cultural heritage—a city that harmonizes its captivating past with an ever-evolving future.

Welcome to Tokyo: An Overview

Tokyo at a Glance:
Japan's capital city of Tokyo is a bustling metropolis that skillfully combines traditional culture with cutting-edge technology. It is one of the most populous cities in the world and serves as the economic, political, and cultural center of Japan. Tokyo is located on the eastern coast of Honshu, the largest island of Japan, and is divided into 23 special wards, each with its own unique charm.

The city offers a wide range of attractions and experiences, from ancient temples and shrines to futuristic skyscrapers and cutting-edge technology. It is known for its efficient public transportation system, cleanliness, and the warm hospitality of its residents. Tokyo hosted the Summer Olympics in 1964 and is set to host the Games again in 2021, showcasing its ability to blend tradition with innovation.

Understanding Japanese Culture:
Traditions and rituals that have been passed down through the centuries are a significant part of Japanese culture. Respect for others, harmony, and attention to detail are important aspects of Japanese society. Here are a few key elements of Japanese culture to keep in mind while visiting Tokyo:

a. Bowing: Bowing is a common form of greeting and showing respect in Japan. The depth of the bow depends on the situation and the status of the person you are interacting with.

b. Etiquette: Japanese etiquette emphasizes politeness and consideration for others.

Removing your shoes before entering someone's home, avoiding loud conversations in public spaces, and using polite language are some examples of Japanese etiquette.

c. Temples and Shrines: Tokyo is home to numerous temples and shrines where you can experience traditional Japanese religious practices. It is important to respect the customs and rules of each place, such as washing your hands before entering and refraining from taking photographs in certain areas.

d. Tea Ceremony: The Japanese tea ceremony, known as "sado" or "chado," is a ceremonial way of preparing and serving matcha (powdered green tea). Participating in a tea ceremony can provide a glimpse into the aesthetics and philosophies of Japanese culture.

Practical Information for Travelers:
Before embarking on your trip to Tokyo, it's helpful to be aware of some practical

information that can enhance your travel experience:

a. Japanese is the official language of Japan. While English is spoken to some extent in tourist areas, it's a good idea to learn a few basic Japanese phrases or carry a translation app to facilitate communication.

b. Currency: The currency used in Japan is the Japanese Yen (JPY). Cash is widely accepted, but credit cards are also commonly used. It's advisable to carry some cash for smaller establishments and vending machines that may not accept cards.

c. Transportation: Tokyo has an extensive and efficient public transportation system, including trains, subways, and buses. The Suica or Pasmo IC cards are convenient for traveling on these systems as they can be used across various modes of transportation.

d. Weather: Tokyo experiences four distinct seasons. Summers (June to August) can be hot and humid, while winters (December to February) are generally mild but can be chilly. Spring (March to May) and autumn (September to November) offer pleasant temperatures and are popular for cherry blossoms and fall foliage, respectively.

e. Safety: Tokyo is considered a safe city, but it's always wise to take standard precautions such as being aware of your surroundings, securing your belongings, and following any safety guidelines provided by local authorities.

By familiarizing yourself with these aspects of Tokyo, you'll be better equipped to immerse yourself in the rich cultural experiences and make the most of your visit to this captivating city.

Expense of travel

If you're considering traveling to Tokyo, you might be concerned about the cost. The capital of Japan is a well-liked tourism attraction that provides visitors with a distinctive cultural encounter. However, traveling to Tokyo can be pricey, making creating a budget for your vacation difficult. I break down the costs involved in traveling to Tokyo, offer advice on how to stick to a spending plan, and offer useful recommendations to help you make the most of your vacation.

Summary of the Cost for a 6-Day, 5-Night Trip to Tokyo

The projected costs for a 6-day, 5-night trip to Tokyo are as follows:

Cost Estimate by Expense Category Flights (roundtrip)
$700 - $1,200
(Hotel) for five nights
$500 - $1,500
(6 days) transportation

$40 - $60

food and beverage

$200 - $300

Entertainment and Activities

$150 - $300

Other Expenses (travel insurance, SIM card, mementos)

$100 - $200

Estimated Total Cost

$1,690 - $3,760

In conclusion, the price of a six-day, five-night trip to Tokyo might vary from $1,690 to $3,760, depending on a number of variables such the type of lodging, available activities, and food alternatives. However, being adaptable and making plans in advance can assist save money and lower the cost of the trip.

Depending on where you depart from and when you travel, the price of flights to Tokyo will change. In general, the most expensive times to fly to Tokyo are the summer and holiday seasons. Consider traveling during the off-season or making your flight reservations far in advance to reduce the cost of your flights.

City Roundtrip Approximate Cost of Flight

Los Angeles to Tokyo in 11 hours, between $600 and $900

From San Francisco Tokyo in 11 hours: $600–$900

from Seattle 11.5 hours in Tokyo, $700 to $1000

City of New York -> 14 hours in Tokyo, $800

Tokyo is a well-liked tourist destination all year round, but the ideal time to go depends on your own preferences and interests.

Due to the well-known cherry blossom season, March, April, and May are very popular with tourists. The city is blanketed in pink and white blooms at this time of year, and many parks and gardens host seasonal festivals and special events.

Tokyo's summers can be hot and muggy, with highs of above 30°C. However, several ancient Japanese events, including the Yasukuni Shrine's Mitama Matsuri and the Sumida River Fireworks Festival, also take place at this time.

A favorite season to visit Tokyo is fall because of the stunning greenery. The parks and gardens are transformed by the changing colors of the leaves. Autumn is a fantastic season to visit the city because of the calm and nice weather.

Tokyo's winters can be frigid, with temperatures occasionally falling below zero. Winter also brings about a number of winter festivities, such as the Odaiba Rainbow Bridge Illumination and the Tokyo Midtown Winter Illumination, and the city is also decked out in Christmas lights.

Overall, your particular preferences and interests will determine the best time to visit Tokyo. Tokyo has lots to offer all year long, whether you prefer the cherry blossoms in spring, the festivals in summer, the fall foliage, or the holiday illuminations.

Transportation

In Tokyo, the expense of transportation can quickly mount, particularly if you intend to use taxis or ride-sharing services. Tokyo does, however, have a robust public transit network that includes trains, buses, and subways. To save money on transportation expenses, think about buying a pre-paid transportation card like a Suica or Pasmo card. Depending on the form of transportation you select and the distance you need to go, transportation costs change in Tokyo. The following are some approximations for Tokyo transportation costs:

Japan Railways (JR) trains and the Tokyo Metro subway system are the most widely used modes of transportation in Tokyo. A single ride can cost anywhere between 160 and 320 yen, depending on the distance covered. For 600 yen, a day pass is good for unlimited travels on the Tokyo Metro; for 1,590 yen, it is good for both JR trains and the Tokyo Metro.

Bus: Another means of transportation in Tokyo is the bus, particularly if you're going somewhere that isn't reachable by train or subway. Tokyo city buses cost 210 yen for a single ride and 500 yen for an unlimited day pass.

Taxis: While more expensive than other forms of transportation, taxis are convenient. Initial ticket is 410 yen, and depending on the time of day, the price each kilometer varies from 80 to 90 yen.

Bicycle: With daily rental costs ranging from 1,000 to 1,500 yen, renting a bicycle is an inexpensive way to move around Tokyo.

Tokyo offers a variety of travel cards that might help you save money on transportation. For instance, the Tokyo Subway Ticket, available for 800, 1,200, or 1,500 yen, provides unlimited travel on the Tokyo Metro and Toei Subway lines for one, two, or three consecutive days. The Tokyo Free Kippu costs 1,590 yen for a day of unrestricted travel on all Tokyo Metro and Toei Subway lines, JR trains within the Tokyo metropolitan area, and city buses.

food and beverages

Depending on where and what you choose to dine, the price of food and drink in Tokyo might vary greatly. Eating at cheap places like izakayas, convenience stores, and ramen cafes can help you save money on meals. Additionally, you can enjoy street food, which is an excellent opportunity to sample regional cuisine without spending a fortune.

Food/Drink
Description Price on average
Sushi
Rice with fresh raw fish on top
2,000–5,000 yen per individual
Ramen noodles in a flavorful broth with a variety of garnishes
750-1,000 yen for each bowl
Okonomiyaki
800–1,500 yen per serving of savory Japanese pancake with pork, fish, and veggies
Octopus balls with flavorful fillings for takoyaki
400–600 yen for each serving
Yakitori
200-300 yen per skewer of grilled chicken
Seafood and vegetables deep-fried in tempura style
1500–3000 yen per serving

Entry criteria and visas

NATIONS & REGIONS EXEMPT FROM JAPANESE VISA
EUROPE
Andorra Macedonia, FYRLithuania Serbia
Austria France Luxembourg Slovakia
Belgium Germany Malta Slovenia
Bulgaria Greece Monaco Spain
Croatia Hungary Netherlands Sweden
Cyprus Iceland Norway Switzerland
Ireland, Czech RepublicPoland British Empire
Denmark Italy Portugal
Estonia Latvia Romania
Finland Liechtenstein Costa Rica
N. AMERICA
Canada the United States
THE CARIBBEAN AND LATIN AMERICA
Argentina Chile South AmericaMexico
Bahamas In Costa RicaGuatemala Surinam Barbados Republic of the DominicaHonduras Uruguay

26

ASIA

Singapore (15 days)Thailand, Republic of (15 days)Macao Indonesia Singapore In Hong KongTaiwan

Malaysia

OCEANIA

Australia In New Zealand

CENTRE EAST

Israel 30 days in the United Arab EmiratesTurkey

AFRICA

Lesotho Tunisia Mauritius

Application for a Japan Tourist Visa and Requirements

You will probably require a Japan tourist visa if you plan to travel to Tokyo.

Millions of tourists flock to Japan each year to experience its unique blend of modernism, culture, history, and nature. Japan is one of the most visited countries in the world.

Although not everyone needs a tourist visa to visit Japan, many of those visitors had to apply for one before they could go.
Who Requires a Japan Tourist Visa?
If you want to travel, visit family or friends, or travel to Japan for another short-term, leisurely reason without the requirement to work for pay, you need a Japan Tourist Visa.

Most nationals in the world must apply for a Japan tourist visa. However, if you reside in one of the aforementioned nations, you are exempt.This means that as long as they are traveling to Japan for tourism, visits, or other short-term, leisurely activities, citizens of those nations—which include those in the EU, the USA, Australia, the UK, etc.—do not need to apply for a visa.

What paperwork do I need to apply for a tourist visa to Japan?
Several supporting documents are required when you apply for a Japanese tourist visa. the following are needed for a tourist visa to

Japan:In this book, we'll talk about how to apply for a tourist visa for Japan.

Application for and Requirements for a Japan Tourist Visa

You'll probably require a Japan tourist visa if you plan to visit Tokyo for leisure.

Japan is one of the most popular tourist destinations in the world, drawing millions of visitors each year who come to experience its unique blend of modernism, culture, history, and environment.

While not all travelers to Japan require a tourist visa, many of those who did had to apply for one before they could visit.

Who Requires a Travel Visa for Japan?

If you wish to travel to Japan, visit family or friends, or travel there for other leisurely and temporary reasons without having to work for money, you need a Japan Tourist Visa.

The majority of international citizens are required to apply for a Japan tourist visa. You are, however, exempt if your country is among those mentioned above.As long as they are traveling to Japan for tourism, visits, or other short-term, leisurely activities, citizens of those nations (which include EU nations, the USA, Australia, the UK, etc.) are not required to apply for a visa.

What supporting documents do I require to apply for a tourist visa to Japan?
You require a number of supporting documents when you apply for a Japanese tourist visa. Following are the prerequisites for a tourist visa to Japan:Japan Tourist Visa Application and Requirements is a separate article.
FAQs and a comprehensive guide to acquiring a Japanese tourist visa.

Japan Visa / Asia / VisaGuide / Tourist Visa
A Japan tourist visa will probably be required if you plan to travel there.

Japan is one of the most popular tourist destinations in the world, drawing millions of visitors each year who come to experience its unique blend of modernism, culture, history, and environment.

While not all travelers to Japan require a tourist visa, many of those who did had to apply for one before they could visit.

Who Requires a Travel Visa for Japan?
If you wish to travel to Japan, visit family or friends, or travel there for other leisurely and temporary reasons without having to work for money, you need a Japan Tourist Visa.

The majority of international citizens are required to apply for a Japan tourist visa. There is a list of nations, nevertheless, whose citizens are exempt from the need for a visa to enter Japan for stays up to 90 days. As long as they are traveling to Japan for tourism, visits, or other short-term, leisurely activities, citizens of those nations (which include EU nations, the USA,

Australia, the UK, etc.) are not required to apply for a visa.

What supporting documents do I require to apply for a tourist visa to Japan?

You require a number of supporting documents when you apply for a Japanese tourist visa. Following are the prerequisites for a tourist visa to Japan:

1. A completed and signed application for a tourist visa to Japan. The Japan Ministry of Foreign Affairs website has a copy of the application form that may be downloaded. Complete every field. Write "N/A" rather than leaving it blank if one doesn't apply to you.

2. Your passport must be at least six months from expiration and have two blank pages available for the visa to be placed in.

self-portraits the size of a passport that meet the requirements stated below

Size: 4.5 cm by 4.5 cm White backdrop

captured throughout the past six months

You must be looking directly ahead while maintaining an expressionless face.

You need to show your complete face.

It must be written on the back with your name and birthdate.

Flight Schedule 3. Include specific information about your arrival and departure times, flight reservation information (you don't have to buy a ticket), your name, etc.

4. Daily Routine. A schedule of your daily activities while visiting Japan must be included. A sample itinerary for a Japan Visa can be found on the website of the Japan Ministry of Foreign Affairs.

5. If your guarantor is located in Japan:

From the Guarantor: A Letter of Invitation

If they'll contribute to the cost of your stay: issued during the last three months are a letter of guarantee and an income certificate.

If they are an overseas Japanese resident, their residence certificate

6.If you are paying for the trip yourself: recent three-month bank statements

Your most recent income tax returns (if you don't have an ITR, you might be able to provide a statement stating why).

If you are visiting a friend or relative, be sure to bring any documentation proving your connection, like:

Civil status records, such as birth or marriage certificates, are required for family members and close friends.

For friends: Photographs of you two, receipts, phone call information, and a letter outlining your friendship

7. If you have a job, a letter of employment from your employer or a no objection certificate.

8. Civil status records, if necessary: birth certificates, marriage licenses, etc.

How to Apply for a Tourist Visa for Japan?

A Japanese Embassy or Consulate overseas is where you must apply for a Japan tourist visa, or you can use a recognized travel agency. The steps involved in applying for a Japan tourist visa can be summed up as follows:

*Make an appointment to submit the application by getting in touch with the Japanese Embassy or Consulate.

However, you must apply through a travel agency since some Japanese Embassies do not accept individual applications. The organization will apply on your behalf at the Embassy or Consulate.

*Acquire the documentation needed for a Japan visa.

*Submit the paperwork at the travel agency or the embassy/consulate.

*Be patient while your visa is processed. From the day your completed application is received by the Japanese Representative Office, this will typically take 5 working days.

*Get your passport from the embassy, consulate, or travel service. If your application is accepted, your visa will be attached, and you can use it to visit Japan within three months of receiving it.

How to obtain a Japan landing permit

After reviewing your Japan tourist visa and the documentation proving your reason for staying, the immigration authorities at the point of entry will issue you a landing permit once you have arrived in Japan.

Your Japan tourist visa will be rendered invalid as soon as you receive the landing permit. For as long as it is valid, you may enter and remain in Japan legally with a Landing Permit (which is stamped on your passport).

How long does it take for a Japanese tourist visa to be processed?
Five working days, beginning on the day the Embassy or Consulate receives your completed application, are required for the processing of a Japanese tourist visa. If they need to send your application to Tokyo's Ministry of Foreign Affairs for additional review or if they need more information from you, this period can be extended.

You must start the application well in advance of the time you want to go in order to prevent delays.

List of international flying companies

Airlines Iberia
The American Airlines
Aloha Airlines
Finnair
Fly France
American Airlines
Airlines United
The airline All Nippon Airways
Airlines Delta
Japanese Airlines (JAL)

Tips for success; What first-time visitors to Japan should do and not do is listed below:

*Avoid inserting chopsticks into rice.
Chopping into rice with chopsticks is a tradition only used during funerals in Japan. It is considered quite impolite to do so elsewhere.
with chopsticks, pointing.
Moving plates or bowls along with them.

meal serving.
using the same end to take shared food and eat it.
giving food to someone else's chopsticks. Furthermore, this is only done at funerals.
Playing with them is viewed negatively by everyone.
*Yes, slurp!Slurp away as much as you like! Just be careful not to make a mess of it.
*When given a gift, accept it.
If at all possible, give gifts in private at the end of the visit.
When delivering or receiving a gift, bow gently and pass the item to the recipient with both hands.
It is customary to say tsumarainai mono desu ga while presenting a gift. Which means "it's boring, but please accept it."
Avoid presenting gifts in sets of four or nine, such as four cupcakes. In Japanese, the number 4 (shi) sounds like the word for death (shinu), and the number 9 (ku) sounds like agony (kurushimi). It seems as though you are wishing the guy misery and death.

*Not a tip. In almost all circumstances outside of establishments run by foreigners, tipping is frowned upon in Japan. Actually, tipping your waiter, hotel, cab driver, etc. is considered rude.

Do's in Tokyo:

1. Do try local street food like takoyaki (octopus balls) and yakitori (grilled skewered meat) from food stalls.
2. Do explore the traditional neighborhoods of Asakusa and Yanaka for a taste of old Tokyo.
3. Do visit a Japanese onsen (hot spring) and follow the bathing etiquette, such as washing thoroughly before entering the baths.
4. Do take off your shoes and use slippers provided when entering traditional ryokans, temples, or certain restaurants.
5. Do experience a traditional tea ceremony to appreciate Japanese tea culture.
6. Do indulge in the vibrant nightlife of areas like Shinjuku and Shibuya, but drink responsibly.

7. Do ride the iconic Tokyo Skytree or Tokyo Tower for breathtaking views of the city.

8. Do follow proper queuing etiquette, especially when waiting for trains or buses.

9. Do take advantage of the efficient public transportation system, including trains and subway networks.

10. Do explore the trendy fashion and shopping districts of Harajuku and Ginza.

11. Do be mindful of others and avoid talking on your phone while using public transportation.

12. Do visit the famous Tsukiji Fish Market for an early morning sushi breakfast.

13. Do try out a karaoke session in a private booth with friends or colleagues.

14. Do visit the Tokyo Disney Resort in Urayasu for a magical experience.

15. Do take part in a traditional Japanese festival if there's one happening during your visit.

Don'ts in Tokyo:

1. Don't eat or drink while riding the subway or trains.
2. Don't stick chopsticks upright in your food, as it resembles a funeral ritual.
3. Don't blow your nose in public; it's considered impolite. Instead, use a handkerchief or tissue.
4. Don't eat or drink while walking on the street, except in designated areas.
5. Don't wear excessive perfume or cologne, as strong scents can be bothersome to others.
6. Don't talk loudly or disturb others in quiet areas, such as temples or libraries.
7. Don't litter—make use of trash cans and separate your trash accordingly.
8. Don't forget to carry a small hand towel or handkerchief to wipe your hands, as some public restrooms may not have paper towels.
9. Don't enter a taxi without closing the door; the driver will usually open and close it for you.
10. Don't touch the displays or merchandise in shops unless given permission to do so.
11. Don't smoke in non-designated areas; use designated smoking spots or smoking rooms.

12. Don't forget to remove your hat or cap when entering religious sites or certain establishments.

13. Don't stick to only touristy areas; explore the lesser-known neighborhoods for a more authentic experience.

14. Don't photograph people without their permission, especially in more intimate settings.

15. Don't forget to carry a phrasebook or use translation apps to help with communication, if needed.

Remember to be mindful of cultural sensitivities and adapt your behavior accordingly. Enjoy your time exploring Tokyo!

Travel insurance

When traveling to Tokyo, it is always a good idea to consider purchasing travel insurance. Travel insurance can help protect you from unexpected expenses and provide assistance in case of emergencies during your trip.

Here are some key points to consider when looking for travel insurance while touring Tokyo:

1. Medical Coverage: Ensure that your travel insurance policy includes sufficient medical coverage for any potential illness or injury you may encounter while in Tokyo. It should cover medical expenses, hospitalization, and emergency medical evacuation if needed.

2. Trip Cancellation and Interruption: Look for a policy that offers coverage for trip cancellation or interruption due to unforeseen circumstances, such as a sudden illness, family emergency, or natural disaster. This coverage can reimburse you for non-refundable expenses like flights, accommodations, and pre-booked activities.

3. Lost or Delayed Baggage: Make sure your travel insurance covers lost, stolen, or delayed baggage. This coverage can help reimburse you for essential items if your luggage is lost or delayed for an extended period.

4. Personal Liability: Check if the policy provides personal liability coverage, which can protect you in case you cause accidental damage to property or injury to someone else while in Tokyo.

5. Emergency Assistance: Look for a policy that includes 24/7 emergency assistance services. This can be helpful if you need assistance with medical referrals, language translation, or arranging emergency transportation.

6. Activities and Excursions: If you plan to engage in adventurous activities or specific excursions while in Tokyo, confirm that your travel insurance policy covers them. Some activities may be excluded or require additional coverage due to their higher risk nature.

7. Pre-existing Conditions: If you have any pre-existing medical conditions, check if your travel insurance covers them. Some policies may have limitations or exclusions for pre-existing

conditions, while others may offer optional coverage at an additional cost.

8. Policy Exclusions: Take the time to read and understand the policy exclusions to know what is not covered. Common exclusions may include self-inflicted injuries, participating in illegal activities, or claims related to alcohol or drug abuse.

Remember to carefully read the terms and conditions of the travel insurance policy and compare multiple options to find the coverage that best suits your needs. It's advisable to purchase travel insurance as soon as you book your trip to ensure coverage for any unexpected events that may occur before or during your time in Tokyo.

Telecommunication

Tokyo is a modern and technologically advanced city with a well-developed telecommunication infrastructure. Here's some information about telecommunication in Tokyo:

1. Mobile Networks: Tokyo has excellent mobile network coverage, and you'll find that major international mobile carriers operate in the city. The primary mobile network technologies used in Tokyo are GSM, 3G, and 4G/LTE. You can purchase a local SIM card or consider renting a portable Wi-Fi device to stay connected while in the city.

2. SIM Cards: Buying a local SIM card is a convenient option for travelers who want to use their own smartphones. Several providers offer prepaid SIM cards specifically designed for tourists. These SIM cards typically provide data, voice, and text messaging services. You can

purchase them at the airports, electronics stores, or designated SIM card retailers in Tokyo.

3. Portable Wi-Fi: Another popular option for staying connected in Tokyo is renting a portable Wi-Fi device (also known as pocket Wi-Fi or mobile hotspot). These devices allow you to connect multiple devices to a secure Wi-Fi network while on the go. Many companies in Tokyo offer portable Wi-Fi rentals, and you can either pick them up at the airport or have them delivered to your accommodation.

4. Public Wi-Fi: Tokyo has an extensive network of free public Wi-Fi hotspots available in various locations, including train stations, airports, shopping malls, cafes, and some public spaces. However, the availability and quality of public Wi-Fi can vary, and some networks may require registration or have usage limitations. It's advisable to have an alternative connectivity option in case you encounter connectivity issues.

5. Internet Cafes: Internet cafes, commonly known as "manga cafes" or "PC bangs," are popular in Tokyo. These establishments provide computer stations with internet access that you can use for a fee. They are convenient if you need to access the internet for a short period or if you don't have your own device.

6. Communication Apps: Many travelers in Tokyo rely on communication apps such as WhatsApp, LINE, or WeChat to stay in touch with friends, family, and fellow travelers. These apps use data or Wi-Fi connections for messaging, voice calls, and video calls. Make sure to have these apps installed on your smartphone before your trip.

7. Payphones: Although payphones are not as common as they used to be, you can still find them in some areas of Tokyo. They accept coins or prepaid telephone cards, which can be purchased at convenience stores or vending machines.

Remember to check with your mobile carrier regarding international roaming rates and compatibility with Japanese networks before traveling to Tokyo. It's also recommended to have a backup plan for connectivity, such as a local SIM card or portable Wi-Fi device, to ensure a reliable internet connection throughout your stay.

The Airalo app

is a mobile application that offers eSIM (embedded SIM) cards for international travelers. It allows users to purchase and manage eSIMs directly from their smartphones, eliminating the need for physical SIM cards or visiting local mobile network providers.

With the Airalo app, users can browse and select eSIMs from various mobile network operators around the world. These eSIMs can be activated instantly, providing users with immediate access to local mobile data and voice services in their destination country. The app also offers data plans for specific regions or countries, allowing users to choose the most suitable option for their needs.

The main advantage of using eSIMs through the Airalo app is the convenience and flexibility it offers. Travelers can avoid the hassle of purchasing and switching physical SIM cards or dealing with roaming charges. Instead, they can conveniently switch between different eSIMs within the app, depending on their location and connectivity requirements.

It's important to note that this information is accurate as of my last knowledge update in September 2021. The Airalo app may have undergone updates or changes since then, so it's recommended to visit the official Airalo website or consult the app's documentation for the most up-to-date information.

Activities for family

Tokyo offers a wide range of family-friendly activities that cater to different interests and age groups. Here are some popular activities for families in Tokyo:

1. Tokyo Disneyland and DisneySea: These iconic theme parks offer a magical experience for the whole family. While DisneySea has a maritime and adventure theme, Tokyo Disneyland contains traditional Disney characters and attractions. Both parks have rides, shows, parades, and character meet-and-greets.

2. Ueno Park: Ueno Park is a large green space with various attractions suitable for families. You can visit Ueno Zoo, one of Japan's oldest and most popular zoos, which houses a diverse range of animals. The park also features museums like the National Museum of Nature and Science, Ueno Royal Museum, and the Tokyo Metropolitan Art Museum.

3. Tokyo Skytree: Head to the Tokyo Skytree, one of the tallest towers in the world, for panoramic views of the city. You can ascend to the observation decks and enjoy breathtaking views of Tokyo's skyline. The Skytree also has a shopping complex, dining options, and an aquarium called Sumida Aquarium.

4. Odaiba: This futuristic entertainment and shopping district has plenty to offer families. You can visit attractions like the teamLab Borderless digital art museum, Palette Town featuring MegaWeb (car theme park), and the Odaiba Seaside Park. Kids will enjoy the interactive exhibits, futuristic technology, and waterfront views.

5. Tokyo Sea Life Park: Located in Kasai Rinkai Park, Tokyo Sea Life Park is a large aquarium with a variety of marine life. It has numerous exhibits showcasing different habitats, including a large tank with dolphins and seals. The park also features touch pools and educational shows.

6. Ghibli Museum: Fans of Studio Ghibli movies will love a visit to the Ghibli Museum in Mitaka. This museum showcases the works of renowned animator Hayao Miyazaki and features exhibits, short films, and a rooftop garden inspired by Ghibli films. Please be aware that prior ticket purchases are required.

7. KidZania Tokyo: KidZania is an interactive indoor theme park where children can role-play various professions, such as doctors, firefighters, chefs, and more. It offers a fun and educational experience for kids to learn about different careers through hands-on activities.

8. Shinjuku Gyoen National Garden: This spacious garden provides a peaceful retreat from the bustling city. Families can have a picnic, stroll through beautifully landscaped gardens, and enjoy the seasonal blooms. There are also open spaces for kids to play.

9. Asakusa: Visit the traditional neighborhood of Asakusa and explore Senso-ji Temple, Tokyo's

oldest Buddhist temple. Take a rickshaw ride, browse the shops in Nakamise Shopping Street, and enjoy the traditional atmosphere. You can also take a river cruise along the Sumida River for a different perspective of Tokyo.

These are just a few examples of family-friendly activities in Tokyo. The city has many more attractions, parks, museums, and entertainment options that cater to families. Consider your children's interests and age when planning activities, and don't forget to check for any specific requirements or restrictions at each venue.

Facts about Tokyo

Certainly! Here are some interesting facts about Tokyo:

1. Capital City: Tokyo is the capital city of Japan and serves as the political, economic, and cultural center of the country. It is one of the most populous cities in the world.

2. Population: Tokyo has a massive population, with over 37 million people in the Greater Tokyo Area, making it the most populous urban area globally.

3. Skyscrapers: Tokyo is renowned for its impressive skyline filled with towering skyscrapers. The Tokyo Skytree is the tallest structure in Japan, standing at 634 meters (2,080 feet) and offers panoramic views of the city.

4. Transportation Hub: Tokyo boasts an extensive and efficient transportation system. It has one of the most extensive urban railway networks, including the famous Tokyo Metro and Japan Railways (JR) lines, making it easy to get around the city.

5. Technology Hub: Tokyo is a major global hub for technology and innovation. It is home to numerous tech companies, electronics manufacturers, and research institutions, contributing to advancements in various fields.

6. Cherry Blossoms: Tokyo is famous for its cherry blossoms, known as sakura in Japanese. Every spring, thousands of cherry trees bloom, and people gather in parks for hanami (flower-viewing) parties to enjoy the picturesque scenes.

7. Temples and Shrines: Despite being a bustling modern metropolis, Tokyo has a rich cultural heritage with numerous temples and shrines scattered throughout the city. Popular ones include Meiji Shrine, Senso-ji Temple, and Yasukuni Shrine.

8. Food Scene: Tokyo is a culinary paradise with a wide array of dining options. It boasts more Michelin-starred restaurants than any other city in the world and offers diverse cuisine, including sushi, ramen, tempura, and many more.

9. Fashion and Shopping: Tokyo is renowned for its fashion and shopping scene. It is a fashion capital, with trendy neighborhoods like Harajuku

and Shibuya offering unique street fashion, high-end boutiques, department stores, and vibrant shopping districts.

10. Safety: Tokyo is considered one of the safest cities in the world, with low crime rates and efficient public safety measures.

These are just a few facts about Tokyo, a city that seamlessly combines tradition and modernity, offering a rich cultural experience alongside technological advancements.

7days itenary

Here's a suggested 7-day itinerary for Tokyo, giving you a mix of cultural, historical, and modern experiences:

Day 1:
- Morning: Explore Asakusa district. Visit Senso-ji Temple, Nakamise Shopping Street, and Asakusa Shrine.

- Afternoon: Take a cruise on the Sumida River and enjoy the scenic views. Visit the Tokyo Skytree for panoramic views of the city.
- Evening: Experience the bustling nightlife in Shibuya. Cross the famous Shibuya Crossing and explore the vibrant streets lined with shops, restaurants, and entertainment venues.

Day 2:
- Morning: Visit the Meiji Shrine in Harajuku, a tranquil Shinto shrine surrounded by a forested area. Explore Takeshita Street, known for its trendy shops and unique fashion.
- Afternoon: Explore Omotesando, a fashionable street with high-end shops, cafes, and architecture. Visit the Nezu Museum, which houses a beautiful collection of Japanese and East Asian art.
- Evening: Head to Shinjuku and visit the Golden Gai area, known for its narrow alleyways filled with tiny bars and eateries. Enjoy the vibrant nightlife in this area.

Day 3:

- Morning: Visit the Tsukiji Fish Market (or Toyosu Fish Market), one of the world's largest seafood markets. Enjoy a fresh sushi breakfast or explore the outer market for food and shopping.
- Afternoon: Explore the upscale neighborhood of Ginza. Visit luxury shops, department stores, and art galleries. Visit a tea establishment to take part in a traditional tea ceremony.
- Evening: Enjoy dinner in one of the many izakayas (Japanese pubs) or try a traditional kaiseki meal for a high-end dining experience.

Day 4:
- Morning: Explore Ueno Park, home to several museums and galleries. Visit the Tokyo National Museum, Ueno Zoo, and Shinobazu Pond.
- Afternoon: Discover the trendy district of Akihabara, known for its electronics shops, anime and manga stores, and gaming centers.
- Evening: Attend a traditional Japanese theater performance, such as Kabuki or Noh, at one of the theaters in the city.

Day 5:
- Morning: Take a day trip to Nikko, a UNESCO World Heritage site located just outside of Tokyo. Explore the Toshogu Shrine, Rinnoji Temple, and the beautiful natural surroundings.
- Afternoon: Visit the Edo-Tokyo Museum to learn about the history and culture of Tokyo. Explore the exhibits showcasing the Edo period and modern Tokyo.
- Evening: Enjoy a relaxing stroll along the waterfront at Odaiba. Visit the Odaiba Seaside Park and enjoy stunning views of the Rainbow Bridge and Tokyo Bay.

Day 6:
- Morning: Explore the trendy neighborhood of Shimokitazawa, known for its vintage clothing stores, indie boutiques, and bohemian atmosphere.
- Afternoon: Visit the teamLab Borderless digital art museum in Odaiba. Immerse yourself in interactive and mesmerizing art installations.
- Evening: Experience traditional Japanese nightlife in the district of Roppongi. Visit one of

the many bars or restaurants for dinner and drinks.

Day 7:
- Morning: Visit the beautiful gardens of the Imperial Palace. Take a walk around the palace grounds and enjoy the serene atmosphere.
- Afternoon: Explore the trendy and artistic neighborhood of Daikanyama. Visit stylish shops, art galleries, and cafes.
- Evening: End your trip with a visit to Tokyo Tower. Enjoy panoramic views of the city from the observation decks and have a farewell dinner at one of the tower's restaurants.

Remember to check the opening hours and any specific reservation requirements for attractions and restaurants in advance, as some places may have limitations or require booking

Festivals and events

Tokyo hosts numerous festivals and events throughout the year, showcasing the city's rich cultural heritage and modern vibrancy.

Here are a few of Tokyo's most significant celebrations and events:

1. Sakura (Cherry Blossom) Season: In late March to early April, Tokyo becomes awash with beautiful cherry blossoms. Parks such as Ueno Park, Shinjuku Gyoen, and Chidorigafuchi are popular spots for hanami (flower viewing) parties.

2. Sumida River Fireworks Festival: Held in late July, this fireworks festival along the Sumida River features stunning displays of fireworks synchronized with music. It attracts millions of spectators each year.

3. Kanda Matsuri: Held every odd-numbered year in mid-May, Kanda Matsuri is one of Tokyo's largest Shinto festivals. It includes parades, processions of portable shrines, and traditional performances around Kanda Myojin Shrine.

4. Tokyo International Film Festival: Taking place in October, this renowned film festival showcases a diverse selection of international and Japanese films, featuring screenings, premieres, and celebrity appearances.

5. Meiji Jingu Autumn Grand Festival: Held annually from late September to early October at Meiji Shrine, this festival features traditional ceremonies, performances, and a parade of portable shrines.

6. Tokyo Game Show: As one of the largest video game exhibitions in the world, the Tokyo Game Show takes place in September. It showcases upcoming video games, technology advancements, and features cosplay events.

7. Tokyo Comic Con: Celebrating pop culture, comics, anime, and gaming, Tokyo Comic Con attracts fans and enthusiasts in early December. The event includes cosplay, merchandise booths, celebrity appearances, and panels.

8. Odaiba Oktoberfest: Inspired by the traditional German beer festival, Odaiba Oktoberfest offers a wide selection of German beers, food, and live music. It typically takes place in late September to early October.

9. Tokyo Jazz Festival: Held in late August or early September, this jazz festival features performances by renowned international and Japanese jazz musicians in various venues across the city.

10. Roppongi Art Night: Taking place annually in late May, Roppongi Art Night is an all-night art event featuring installations, exhibitions, live performances, and interactive art projects throughout Roppongi district.

These are just a few examples of the festivals and events that take place in Tokyo. It's always a good idea to check the specific dates and details for each event as they may vary from year to year. Additionally, Tokyo hosts many other cultural, culinary, and sports events throughout the year, offering a diverse range of experiences for visitors and locals alike.

Packing list

When preparing for a trip to Tokyo, it's important to consider the season, activities planned, and personal preferences. However, here's a general packing list to help you get started:

1. Clothing:
- Comfortable walking shoes
- Lightweight, breathable clothing (T-shirts, shorts, skirts, dresses)
- Light jacket or sweater for cooler evenings (depending on the season)
- Raincoat or umbrella (Tokyo can experience rain throughout the year)
- Swimsuit (if you plan to visit hot springs or water parks)
- Hat or cap for sun protection
- Socks and underwear
- Sleepwear

2. Travel Essentials:
- Passport and other travel documents
- electrical device charger and travel adapter
- Portable battery pack for recharging devices on the go
- Mobile phone and charger
- Camera or smartphone for capturing memories
- Cash and credit/debit cards
- Language translation app or pocket dictionary
- Travel guidebook or maps

3. Toiletries and Medications:
- Toothbrush, toothpaste, and dental floss
- Shampoo, conditioner, and body wash (you can also find these in hotels or convenience stores)
- Skincare products (moisturizer, sunscreen, lip balm)
- Personal medications and prescriptions
- Basic first aid kit (band-aids, pain relievers, motion sickness medication)
- Hand sanitizer and wet wipes

4. Electronics and Entertainment:

- Laptop or tablet (if needed)
- E-reader or books for leisurely reading
- Headphones or earphones for music and entertainment
- Portable Wi-Fi device or SIM card for internet access (if necessary)
- Travel journal and pen

5. Miscellaneous Items:
- Travel lock for securing your luggage
- Travel pillow and eye mask for comfortable flights or train rides
- Reusable water bottle
- Snacks for the journey
- Foldable tote bag or backpack for carrying souvenirs
- Travel umbrella
- Coin bag
- A small bag to keep your trash as there are hardly any trash can

Remember to check the weather forecast before your trip and make any necessary adjustments to your packing list. Additionally, consider the specific activities you plan to engage in, such as hiking or attending formal events, and pack accordingly.

Rules for taking photos

When taking photos in Tokyo, it's important to be mindful of the local customs and regulations. Following are some general principles:

1. Respect privacy: Avoid taking photos of individuals without their permission, particularly close-ups. It's polite to ask for consent before photographing people, especially in intimate or private settings.

2. Follow signs and guidelines: Some areas in Tokyo may have restrictions on photography or require permits for commercial shoots. Respect any signage indicating photography restrictions, such as in museums, galleries, or certain public spaces.

3. Be considerate in crowded areas: Tokyo is a bustling city with many popular tourist spots. When taking photos in crowded places, be mindful of others around you. Avoid obstructing pathways or causing inconvenience to fellow visitors.

4. Respect cultural and religious sites: When visiting shrines, temples, or other religious sites, be mindful of their sanctity and the religious

practices taking place. Some areas may have designated photography-free zones or specific rules regarding photography. Follow any instructions provided and be respectful of worshippers.

5. Exercise caution with street photography: While Tokyo offers many photogenic streets and urban scenes, be aware of the privacy of individuals and businesses. Avoid taking photos of people without their consent or invading their personal space.

6. Ask permission for specific subjects: If you wish to photograph street performers, street vendors, or individuals in traditional attire (like geisha or maiko), it's polite to ask for permission first. Respect their decision if they decline or request a fee for photography.

7. Follow the rules of specific attractions: Different tourist attractions in Tokyo may have their own photography rules. Some may allow photography throughout, while others may have restricted areas or prohibit photography altogether. Follow the guidelines provided by the attraction.

8. Use discretion in sensitive areas: Some areas, such as government buildings, military installations, or certain neighborhoods, may have restrictions on photography. Exercise caution and follow any instructions or signage provided.

9. Be mindful of local customs: Tokyo is a city with rich cultural traditions. Be respectful of local customs, especially during festivals,

ceremonies, or traditional events. Ask for permission before photographing individuals participating in such activities.

Remember, these guidelines are meant to ensure respectful and responsible photography in Tokyo. Always be aware of your surroundings and show consideration for the people and places you are capturing in your photos.

Transportation in Tokyo

we will provide you with essential information on how to navigate Tokyo's transportation system, ensuring a seamless and efficient journey through the city. From the extensive subway system to alternative transportation options, let's explore the various ways to get around Tokyo.

. Navigating the Subway System:

Tokyo's subway system is renowned for its efficiency, reliability, and extensive coverage. Here are some key points to help you navigate the subway system:

a. Tokyo Metro and Toei Subway: Tokyo's subway system is divided into two main operators: Tokyo Metro and Toei Subway. Both networks have interconnected lines, providing comprehensive coverage throughout the city.

b. Subway Maps and Apps: Obtain a subway map from the station or download a reliable subway navigation app on your smartphone. These maps and apps provide detailed route information, station names in English, and estimated travel times.

c. Fare Payment: To ride the subway, you can purchase tickets from vending machines at the stations. Alternatively, consider getting a prepaid IC card (Suica or Pasmo) for convenient fare payment across various modes of transportation.

d. Rush Hour Considerations: Tokyo's subway can get crowded during peak hours, especially on weekdays between 7:30 am and 9:00 am, and in the late afternoon. If possible, plan your travel outside of these peak periods to avoid crowded trains.

Public Transportation Options:
In addition to the subway system, Tokyo offers a range of public transportation options to explore the city. Here are a few alternatives:

a. JR Yamanote Line: The JR Yamanote Line is a circular rail line that loops around central Tokyo, stopping at major stations like Tokyo, Shinjuku, Shibuya, and Ueno. It is especially convenient for accessing popular tourist areas.

b. Buses: Tokyo has an extensive bus network that covers areas not served by the subway. Buses are a great option for sightseeing and reaching specific destinations. Be sure to have the correct fare ready when boarding or use your IC card.

c. Taxis: Taxis are readily available in Tokyo, but they tend to be more expensive compared to other modes of transportation. Taxis are a convenient option for short trips or when traveling with heavy luggage.

d. Trains: In addition to the subway and JR lines, Tokyo has regional train lines that connect the city to neighboring areas and attractions. For example, the Keio Line provides access to the popular suburb of Mount Takao.

Renting Bicycles and Other Transportation Tips: Exploring Tokyo on a bicycle can be a fun and convenient way to discover the city's neighborhoods. Many rental services offer bicycles for short-term use. Keep the following tips in mind:

a. Bicycle Rentals: Look for bicycle rental shops, especially near parks and tourist areas. Some hotels and guesthouses also offer bicycle rentals for their guests.

b. Cycling Etiquette: Observe traffic rules, ride on designated cycling lanes or sidewalks, and be mindful of pedestrians. Park your bicycle in designated areas to avoid inconveniencing others.

c. Walking: Tokyo is a pedestrian-friendly city, and walking can be a great way to explore specific areas, especially those with narrow streets and unique shops.

d. Transportation Passes: Consider purchasing a transportation pass like the Tokyo Subway Ticket or Tokyo Free Kippu. These passes offer unlimited rides on subways, trains, and buses within a specified period, providing cost-effective options for extensive travel.

e. Accessibility: Tokyo's public transportation system is generally accessible for individuals with disabilities, with elevators and ramps available in many stations. However, it's important to note that not all stations may have full accessibility features, especially older or smaller stations. Here are some points to consider regarding accessibility:

- Elevators and Escalators: Most major stations in Tokyo have elevators or escalators to facilitate easy access to platforms. Look for signs indicating elevator locations or ask station staff for assistance.

- Barrier-Free Routes: Tokyo Metro and Toei Subway provide barrier-free routes in their stations, guiding passengers with disabilities through accessible pathways. These routes are marked with symbols and signs, ensuring smooth navigation.

- Assistance from Station Staff: Station staff members are generally helpful and ready to assist passengers with disabilities. They can provide information on accessible routes, offer guidance, or provide wheelchair assistance when needed.

- Priority Seating: Tokyo's trains and buses have designated priority seating areas for elderly individuals, pregnant women, and passengers with disabilities. These seats are marked with signs and should be offered to those who need them. However, it's important to note that not all passengers may be aware or adhere to this etiquette.

- Guide Dogs: Guide dogs are permitted on Tokyo's public transportation systems, including trains, subways, and buses. However, it's recommended to have the dog in a harness or with identifying tags to avoid any confusion.

- Portable Ramps: Some stations may provide portable ramps upon request for passengers using wheelchairs or mobility devices. It's advisable to contact the station in advance or inquire with station staff for assistance.

- Accessibility Apps and Resources: There are mobile apps and online resources available that provide information on accessible routes, facilities, and services in Tokyo. These resources can assist individuals with disabilities in planning their travel and navigating the city more easily.

It's worth noting that Tokyo is continuously working towards improving accessibility in public transportation. However, it's recommended to plan your routes in advance, familiarize yourself with accessible stations, and reach out to station staff if you require any assistance during your journey.

By considering these transportation options and tips, you'll be well-equipped to navigate Tokyo's diverse and efficient transportation system, ensuring a smooth and enjoyable experience as you explore the city.

The Suica card

is a rechargeable smart card used for transportation in Tokyo and other major cities in Japan. It is primarily used for train travel, but it can also be used for buses, subways, and some taxis. The Suica card is issued by the East Japan Railway Company (JR East) and is part of a larger smart card system called "IC cards" (Integrated Circuit cards).

Here are some key points about the Suica card:

1. Usage: The Suica card allows for convenient and cashless travel on various modes of transportation. Instead of buying individual

tickets, you can simply touch the card on the reader at the ticket gates or on buses to pay for your fare. The fare is automatically deducted from the card's balance.

2. Rechargeability: The Suica card is rechargeable, which means you can add money to it whenever your balance is low. You can recharge the card at ticket vending machines, Suica-compatible ticket offices, or through automated recharge machines at train stations. Online recharge options are also available.

3. Integration: The Suica card is part of a larger network of IC cards in Japan, including PASMO, ICOCA, and others. This means that if you have any of these cards, they are interoperable and can be used interchangeably on most transportation systems across the country.

4. Widespread acceptance: The Suica card is widely accepted in Tokyo and other major cities, including Osaka, Kyoto, and Sapporo. You can use it on trains operated by JR East, as well as

other railways, subways, and buses that accept IC cards.

5. Beyond transportation: In addition to transportation, the Suica card can also be used for various non-transportation purposes. It can be used to make small purchases at certain vending machines, convenience stores, supermarkets, and some other retailers that display the Suica logo.

6. Suica App: JR East offers a mobile app called "Suica App" that allows you to manage your Suica card, recharge it, view your usage history, and even use it for mobile payments through compatible smartphones or smartwatches.

The Suica card is a convenient and popular option for residents and visitors in Tokyo who frequently use public transportation. It eliminates the need to buy individual tickets and offers a seamless travel experience across multiple modes of transportation.

Car rental companies

Here are some car rental companies in Tokyo along with an approximate price range for reference. Please note that the prices mentioned are general estimates and can vary based on factors such as rental duration, vehicle type, seasonal demand, and additional services:

1. Toyota Rent a Car: Toyota Rent a Car offers a wide range of vehicles starting from compact cars to larger models like minivans and SUVs. Prices can vary depending on the vehicle and rental duration, but as a general estimate, daily rates may range from ¥5,000 to ¥15,000 (approximately $45 to $135).

2. Nissan Rent a Car: Nissan Rent a Car provides various car models, including economy cars, hybrids, and electric vehicles. Daily rental rates may range from ¥4,000 to ¥12,000 (approximately $35 to $110), depending on the vehicle type and rental period.

3. Times Car Rental: Times Car Rental offers a diverse selection of vehicles, including compact cars, sedans, and SUVs. Daily rental rates can range from ¥3,000 to ¥10,000 (approximately $27 to $90), with prices varying based on the vehicle category and rental duration.

4. ORIX Rent a Car: ORIX Rent a Car provides a range of vehicles, from compact cars to minivans and luxury cars. Daily rates can range from ¥4,000 to ¥15,000 (approximately $35 to $135) or more, depending on the vehicle type and rental period.

5. Budget Rent a Car: Budget Rent a Car offers affordable rates for various car categories. Daily rental prices can range from ¥3,000 to ¥10,000 (approximately $27 to $90), depending on the vehicle size, rental duration, and any additional services or options selected.

6. Nippon Rent a Car: Nippon Rent a Car provides a variety of vehicles, including economy cars, sedans, and larger models

suitable for families or groups. Daily rates may range from ¥4,000 to ¥12,000 (approximately $35 to $110), with prices varying based on the vehicle category and rental period.

Please note that these price ranges are approximate and can vary depending on the factors mentioned earlier. It's advisable to check with the specific car rental company for the most accurate and up-to-date pricing information based on your travel dates and requirements.

Accommodation Options

we will explore various accommodation options available in Tokyo, ranging from luxurious hotels to budget-friendly guesthouses. Whether you seek a traditional experience or modern comforts, Tokyo offers a diverse range of choices to suit every traveler's needs.

Hotels and Ryokans:
Tokyo boasts a plethora of hotels that cater to a wide range of budgets and preferences. From luxurious international chains to boutique accommodations, here are some key points to consider:

- Luxury Hotels: Tokyo is home to numerous five-star hotels that offer world-class amenities, elegant rooms, and exceptional services. These establishments often feature multiple restaurants, spas, fitness centers, and stunning city views.

- Business Hotels: Tokyo also has a wide selection of business hotels that provide comfortable rooms, essential amenities, and convenient locations near major business districts and transportation hubs. These hotels are often more affordable compared to luxury options.

- Ryokans: For those seeking a traditional Japanese experience, staying in a ryokan is a must. Ryokans are traditional inns that feature tatami mat floors, futon beds, communal baths, and exquisite kaiseki (multi-course) meals. Some ryokans in Tokyo offer a blend of traditional and modern elements, catering to both local and international guests.

Guesthouses and Hostels:
If you are looking for budget-friendly options or a more social atmosphere, guesthouses and hostels are excellent choices in Tokyo. Here are some key features:

- Guesthouses: Guesthouses in Tokyo typically offer private rooms or dormitory-style accommodations. They often provide communal spaces, such as shared kitchens, lounges, and common areas, where guests can interact and share experiences. These establishments are a great option for solo travelers, backpackers, or those looking to connect with fellow adventurers.

- Hostels: Tokyo has a variety of hostels that offer affordable dormitory-style accommodations with shared facilities. Many hostels provide communal spaces, such as common rooms, cafes, or bars, where guests can socialize and relax. Hostels are popular among young travelers, students, and backpackers.

Traditional Japanese Inns (Minshuku):
In addition to ryokans, Tokyo also offers traditional Japanese inns known as minshuku. Here are some key features:

- Minshuku: Minshuku are family-run accommodations that provide a more intimate and homely experience. These inns often have a limited number of rooms and are typically found in residential neighborhoods or rural areas. Minshuku offer comfortable rooms, home-cooked meals, and a chance to interact closely with local hosts, immersing yourself in Japanese hospitality.

- Shared Facilities: Minshuku may have shared facilities such as communal baths or dining areas, allowing guests to experience a sense of community and connect with other travelers.

When choosing accommodation in Tokyo, consider factors such as location, budget, amenities, and the experience you desire. It's advisable to book your accommodations in advance, especially during peak travel seasons, to ensure availability and secure the best rates.

Remember to check for reviews, compare prices, and consider the proximity to major attractions or transportation options to make the most of your stay in Tokyo

Depending on interest and budget recommended places to stay

Tokyo offers a wide range of accommodation options to suit different interests and budgets. Here are some recommendations based on various preferences:

1. Shinjuku: This bustling district is a popular choice for travelers due to its convenient location, vibrant nightlife, and abundance of shops and restaurants. There are many accommodation options available, ranging from budget-friendly capsule hotels to luxury hotels.

2. Shibuya: Known for its trendy atmosphere and iconic Shibuya Crossing, Shibuya is a great choice for those looking to immerse themselves in Tokyo's youth culture. You can find a variety of accommodation options, including budget hotels and stylish boutique hotels.

3. Asakusa: If you prefer a more traditional and historical experience, Asakusa is an excellent choice. It is home to Senso-ji Temple and offers a glimpse into old Tokyo. You can find ryokans (traditional Japanese inns) and budget-friendly guesthouses in this area.

4. Ginza: For those interested in luxury shopping and upscale dining experiences, Ginza is a prime location. This district is known for its high-end department stores, designer boutiques, and Michelin-starred restaurants. There are several luxury hotels in this area.

5. Roppongi: Roppongi is a popular nightlife and entertainment district, with many clubs, bars, and international restaurants. It also has a thriving art scene and is home to several art museums. There are various accommodation options, including luxury hotels and serviced apartments.

6. Ueno: Ueno is a vibrant district with a mix of cultural attractions, including Ueno Park,

museums, and a zoo. It offers a range of accommodation options, from budget hotels to mid-range hotels.

7. Akihabara: Known as the electronics and anime district, Akihabara is a haven for tech enthusiasts and anime fans. It also offers a unique and vibrant atmosphere. You can find a variety of accommodation options, including budget-friendly capsule hotels and business hotels.

8. Ikebukuro: Ikebukuro is a bustling district with shopping malls, entertainment centers, and a lively nightlife. It is also home to the Sunshine City complex, which includes an aquarium, observation deck, and shopping facilities. There are hotels catering to different budgets in this area.

When choosing accommodation, consider factors such as location, proximity to public transportation, and your budget. It's advisable to book in advance, especially during peak travel seasons, to secure your preferred choice of accommodation.

Booking advice and popular lodging choices

When it comes to booking accommodation in Tokyo, here are some tips and popular lodging choices:

1. Book in Advance: Tokyo is a busy city with a high demand for accommodation, so it's advisable to book your lodging well in advance, especially during peak travel seasons or for popular events. Booking early ensures you have a wider selection of options and better rates.

2. Consider Location: Tokyo is a vast city with multiple neighborhoods offering different experiences. Consider the areas that align with your interests and activities. Look for accommodations near convenient transportation

hubs, such as train stations, to easily navigate the city.

3. Budget Accommodation: If you're on a budget, Tokyo offers various budget-friendly options. Capsule hotels, hostels, and guesthouses are popular choices for affordable accommodations. Look for well-reviewed and centrally located options to maximize convenience.

4. Business Hotels: Tokyo has a wide range of business hotels that cater to both business and leisure travelers. These hotels often offer comfortable rooms with essential amenities at reasonable prices. They are generally well-located and provide convenient access to transportation.

5. Ryokans: For a traditional Japanese experience, consider staying at a ryokan. These are traditional inns that offer tatami-matted rooms, futon beds, and Japanese-style baths. Ryokans can be found in areas like Asakusa and

are a great way to immerse yourself in Japanese culture.

6. Luxury Hotels: Tokyo boasts numerous luxury hotels that provide exceptional service, world-class amenities, and stunning views. Popular luxury hotels can be found in upscale areas such as Ginza, Roppongi, and Shinjuku.

7. Apartment Rentals: Another option to consider is renting an apartment or serviced apartment. This can be a great choice for longer stays or if you prefer a more homely environment. Websites and platforms like Airbnb offer a variety of apartment rentals in Tokyo.

8. Hotel Chains: International hotel chains such as Hilton, Marriott, and Hyatt have a strong presence in Tokyo. These hotels offer consistent service, comfortable rooms, and loyalty programs that can be beneficial if you frequently stay with these chains.

When booking, read reviews and check the amenities, cancellation policies, and proximity to public transportation. Consider your specific needs and preferences to choose the best lodging option for your stay in Tokyo.

Accommodation & prices

Accommodation in Tokyo can be expensive, with hotel rooms costing upwards of $200 per night. However, there are budget-friendly options available, such as hostels, guesthouses, and Airbnb rentals. Consider staying in a budget-friendly accommodation option, such as a capsule hotel, to save money on lodging.

Top 5 Tokyo Hotels

Tokyo is a city of contrasts, where ancient traditions blend seamlessly with modern technology. For those planning a trip to Tokyo, here are the top 5 hotels that offer the perfect combination of comfort, convenience, and luxury:

1. Mandarin Oriental, Tokyo

Address: Nihonbashi Muromachi 2-1-1 Chuo-ku, Tokyo.Located in the heart of the bustling city, this hotel boasts stunning views of the Tokyo skyline. The rooms are elegant and spacious, with a minimalist design that creates a serene atmosphere. The hotel features a spa, fitness center, and several restaurants, including the Michelin-starred Signature restaurant. Prices start at around $500 per night.

2. Park Hyatt Tokyo

Address: 3-7-1-2 Nishi Shinjuku, Shinjuku-ku, Tokyo.This iconic hotel is situated in the heart of Shinjuku and is renowned for its panoramic views of the city. The rooms are designed with a contemporary aesthetic, with floor-to-ceiling windows that offer spectacular views. The hotel features a fitness center, indoor pool, and several dining options, including the Michelin-starred New York Grill. Prices start at around $500 per night.

3. Aman Tokyo

Address: 1-5-6 Otemachi, Chiyoda-ku, Tokyo.This luxury hotel is located in the Otemachi district, offering a tranquil retreat in the heart of the city. The rooms feature a Japanese aesthetic, with sliding doors and traditional wooden furnishings. The hotel has a spa, fitness center, and several dining options, including the Michelin-starred Arva restaurant. Prices start at around $1000 per night.

4. The Peninsula Tokyo

Address: 1-8-1 Yurakucho, Chiyoda-ku, Tokyo.This hotel is situated in the Marunouchi district, offering easy access to the city's attractions. The rooms are designed with a modern aesthetic, with neutral tones and sleek furnishings. The hotel features a spa, fitness center, and several dining options, including the Michelin-starred restaurant, Peter. Prices start at around $500 per night.

5. The Ritz-Carlton, Tokyo

Address: Tokyo Midtown, 9-7-1 Akasaka, Minato-ku, Tokyo.This hotel is located in the upscale Roppongi district, offering stunning views of the Tokyo skyline. The rooms are spacious and elegant, with a contemporary design that exudes luxury. The hotel has a spa, fitness center, and several dining options, including the Michelin-starred restaurant, Azure 45. Prices start at around $500 per night.

Note:Each of these hotels offers a unique experience, from modern luxury to traditional Japanese aesthetics. No matter which one you choose, you are sure to have an unforgettable stay in Tokyo.

.

Dining in Tokyo

we will delve into the culinary delights of Tokyo, exploring the must-try Japanese dishes, the vibrant sushi bars and izakayas, and the unique dining experiences offered by themed cafes. Get ready to embark on a gastronomic adventure through the diverse flavors of Tokyo.

 Must-Try Japanese Dishes:
Tokyo is a paradise for food lovers, offering a wide array of traditional Japanese dishes. Here are some must-try culinary delights:

- Sushi: Indulge in the art of sushi, where fresh fish or other ingredients are delicately placed on bite-sized morsels of vinegared rice. Visit renowned sushi establishments, such as Tsukiji Fish Market or the upscale sushi restaurants in Ginza, for an unforgettable sushi experience.

- Ramen: Savor a steaming bowl of ramen, a hearty noodle soup dish with various regional variations. Whether you prefer the rich and creamy tonkotsu ramen or the flavorful shoyu ramen, you can find exceptional ramen shops throughout Tokyo, with popular areas including Ikebukuro and Shinjuku.

- Tempura: Enjoy the light and crispy delight of tempura, where battered and deep-fried seafood, vegetables, and other ingredients are served with a dipping sauce. Experience the exquisite tempura at specialized restaurants like Tenkuni or try the tempura bars in the upscale department stores.

- Yakitori: Delight in skewered and grilled chicken at yakitori establishments. From tender chicken meat to succulent organs, yakitori offers a range of flavorful options. Explore the vibrant alleys of Yakitori Alley in Shinjuku or visit traditional izakayas for an authentic yakitori experience.

- Okonomiyaki: Try okonomiyaki, a savory pancake filled with various ingredients like cabbage, meat, seafood, and topped with a tangy sauce and mayonnaise. Head to the bustling neighborhood of Tsukishima or Okonomiyaki Street in Asakusa for mouthwatering variations of this beloved dish.

Sushi Bars and Izakayas:
Tokyo is renowned for its sushi bars and izakayas, offering unique dining experiences. Here's what to expect:

- Sushi Bars: Immerse yourself in the world of sushi at traditional sushi bars, where skilled sushi chefs meticulously prepare and serve the freshest seafood. Enjoy the intimate ambiance, sit at the counter, and witness the chef's culinary mastery. Popular sushi bars include Sukiyabashi Jiro (Ginza) and Sushi Dai (Tsukiji).

- Izakayas: Discover the lively atmosphere of izakayas, Japanese-style pubs where you can enjoy drinks and a variety of small, flavorful dishes. Order a range of dishes to share, such as yakitori, sashimi, and grilled skewers, while sipping on sake or Japanese beer. Explore the izakaya alleys of Shinjuku's Omoide Yokocho or the vibrant district of Golden Gai.

Themed Cafes and Unique Dining Experiences: Tokyo takes dining to another level with its themed cafes and unique dining experiences. Here are some extraordinary options:

- Animal Cafes: Tokyo is famous for its animal cafes, where you can enjoy a cup of coffee or tea in the company of furry friends. Visit cat cafes, owl cafes, or hedgehog cafes for a memorable and relaxing experience.

-Maid Cafes: Enter the world of fantasy and charm at maid cafes, where waitresses dressed in maid costumes provide attentive service. Enjoy cute and themed dishes while being entertained by the maids who often perform songs, dances, and interactive games. Maid cafes, such as Maidreamin in Akihabara, offer a unique and playful dining experience that is popular among anime and manga enthusiasts.

- Robot Restaurants: Step into a futuristic realm at Tokyo's robot restaurants, where dazzling performances featuring robots, lights, and music take center stage. Enjoy a multi-course meal while being mesmerized by the high-energy spectacle. The Robot Restaurant in Shinjuku is a popular destination for this one-of-a-kind dining experience.

- Kaiseki Dining: Indulge in the refined art of kaiseki, a traditional multi-course dining experience that showcases seasonal ingredients and meticulous presentation. Kaiseki restaurants, like the renowned Ishikawa in Kagurazaka, offer a journey through the essence of Japanese cuisine, where every dish is thoughtfully crafted and harmonized.

- Food Markets: Explore Tokyo's bustling food markets, such as Tsukiji Fish Market or Ameya-Yokocho Market, to immerse yourself in the vibrant local food culture. Sample fresh seafood, street snacks, and a variety of local delicacies, experiencing the lively atmosphere and flavors that Tokyo has to offer.

- Food Districts: Discover Tokyo's diverse food districts, each with its own specialty and culinary offerings. Visit the historic district of Yanaka for traditional street food, explore the food stalls of Yurakucho's Gado-shita under the railway tracks, or savor the international cuisine of Shibuya or Shin-Okubo's Korean Town.

- Depachika: Delight in the basement food halls, known as depachika, found in many department stores across Tokyo. These gourmet wonderlands offer an array of high-quality foods, including bento boxes, pastries, sweets, and regional specialties. Explore depachika in popular shopping areas like Ginza or Shibuya for a delightful culinary experience.

When dining in Tokyo, keep in mind that reservations are recommended for popular or high-end establishments. Additionally, it's essential to familiarize yourself with basic

Japanese dining etiquette, such as saying "Itadakimasu" before the meal and "Gochisousama deshita" after finishing. Embrace the culinary diversity and unique dining experiences that Tokyo has to offer, and savor the flavors that make the city a food lover's paradise.

By exploring the must-try Japanese dishes, sushi bars, izakayas, themed cafes, and unique dining experiences, you'll embark on a culinary journey that will leave you with lasting memories of Tokyo's vibrant food scene.

Popular eateries,rates and restaurants

Tokyo is known for its diverse and vibrant food scene, offering a wide range of culinary experiences. While it's difficult to provide specific rates for individual eateries and restaurants, here are some popular categories and price ranges to give you an idea of what to expect when dining out in Tokyo:

1. Street Food and Casual Eateries:
   - Street food stalls and food carts: Prices can range from ¥500 to ¥1,500 (approximately $4.50 to $13.50) per item.
   - Ramen shops: A bowl of ramen typically costs around ¥800 to ¥1,500 (approximately $7 to $13.50), depending on the shop and ingredients.
   - Conveyor belt sushi (kaiten-zushi): Prices per plate often range from ¥100 to ¥500 (approximately $0.90 to $4.50) with different colors representing various prices.

2. Mid-Range Restaurants:
   - Izakayas (Japanese gastropubs): Average costs per person may range from ¥2,500 to ¥5,000 (approximately $22.50 to $45) depending on the number of dishes ordered and drinks consumed.
   - Casual Japanese restaurants: Prices can vary, but a set meal or a la carte dishes may range

from ¥1,500 to ¥3,500 (approximately $13.50 to $31.50) per person.

- Western-style cafes and restaurants: Prices can vary widely, but a meal may typically cost around ¥1,500 to ¥3,500 (approximately $13.50 to $31.50) per person.

3. Fine Dining and High-End Restaurants:

- High-end sushi restaurants: Omakase (chef's choice) meals can range from ¥15,000 to ¥40,000 (approximately $135 to $360) or more per person.

- Michelin-starred restaurants: Prices vary greatly depending on the restaurant and the number of courses. Expect to pay anywhere from ¥10,000 to ¥50,000 (approximately $90 to $450) or more per person.

It's important to note that these price ranges are estimates, and actual costs can vary depending on factors such as the specific restaurant, location, menu choices, and seasonal fluctuations. Additionally, some restaurants may have additional charges like seating fees or service charges, especially in high-end establishments.

Tokyo offers a wide range of dining options to suit different budgets, tastes, and preferences. Exploring local neighborhoods, trying street food, and visiting local markets are great ways to discover affordable and delicious food options.

Tokyo is a culinary paradise with a vast range of dining options, from street food stalls to high-end restaurants. While it's difficult to provide specific rates for each eatery or restaurant, I can give you an overview of the dining scene and popular dining areas in Tokyo:

Street Food: In bustling areas like Shibuya, Shinjuku, and Asakusa, you'll find street food stalls and vendors offering a variety of affordable snacks and quick bites. Prices for street food can range from ¥300 to ¥800 (approximately $3 to $7) per item.

Ramen Shops: Tokyo is known for its delicious ramen. Ramen shops can vary in price, but a basic bowl of ramen typically costs between ¥800 to ¥1,500 (approximately $7 to $13). Some popular ramen areas include Ikebukuro, Shinjuku, and Tokyo Station.

Conveyor Belt Sushi: For an affordable sushi experience, try conveyor belt sushi (kaiten-zushi) restaurants. Prices per plate usually range from ¥100 to ¥500 (approximately $1 to $4.50), and you can enjoy a variety of sushi options.

Izakayas: Izakayas are traditional Japanese pubs where you can enjoy a wide selection of small dishes and drinks. Prices can vary depending on the establishment, but expect to pay around ¥2,000 to ¥4,000 (approximately $18 to $36) per person for a satisfying meal.

Yokocho Alleys: Yokocho alleys are narrow, atmospheric lanes lined with small eateries and bars. Areas like Omoide Yokocho in Shinjuku and Piss Alley in Shibuya offer a glimpse into the old-style dining experience. Prices for food and drinks can range from ¥500 to ¥3,000 (approximately $4.50 to $27) per item.

High-End Dining: Tokyo is home to numerous high-end and Michelin-starred restaurants. Prices in upscale establishments can vary significantly depending on the restaurant, cuisine, and menu. Expect to pay several thousand yen per person for a multi-course meal at high-end restaurants.

Department Store Basements: Tokyo's department stores often have impressive food basements (depachika) offering a wide selection of gourmet food, bento boxes, pastries, and more. Prices can vary, but you can find reasonably priced options starting from around 500 yen ($4.50) and going up to more expensive gourmet items. Some popular department stores with renowned food basements in Tokyo include:

1. Mitsukoshi Department Store (Ginza): Mitsukoshi's depachika is famous for its high-quality food products, including fresh seafood, sushi, wagyu beef, and a variety of traditional Japanese sweets and snacks.

2. Isetan Department Store (Shinjuku): Isetan's depachika is known for its wide range of international and Japanese food offerings. You can find everything from French pastries and Italian deli items to sushi and bento boxes.

3. Takashimaya Department Store (Nihonbashi): Takashimaya has an extensive food basement with various stalls offering sushi, tempura, teppanyaki, and other Japanese delicacies. They also have a section dedicated to regional Japanese specialties.

4. Tokyu Food Show (Shibuya): Located in the basement of Tokyu Department Store, Tokyu Food Show is a popular gourmet food market offering a diverse selection of Japanese and international cuisines. You can find everything

from sushi and sashimi to Italian pasta and French pastries.

5. Odakyu Department Store (Shinjuku): Odakyu's depachika is known for its wide range of food products and sweets. They offer a variety of bentos, sushi, cakes, and desserts, catering to different tastes and budgets.

These department store basements are not only great places to grab a quick and delicious meal but also perfect for picking up souvenirs or exploring the local culinary scene. Prices can vary depending on the specific items and vendors, but there are usually options to suit different budgets.

Choices for vegetarians and vegans

Tokyo has a growing number of options for vegetarians and vegans, and you can find various restaurants and cafes that cater specifically to plant-based diets. Here are some choices for vegetarians and vegans in Tokyo:

1. T's Tantan: Located in Tokyo Station, T's Tantan is a popular vegan ramen restaurant. They offer delicious and flavorful ramen dishes made with plant-based ingredients, including their signature tantanmen.

2. Ain Soph Ripple: Ain Soph Ripple is a vegan cafe located in Shinjuku. They offer a wide range of vegan dishes, including burgers, sandwiches, pasta, and desserts. Their menu features both Western and Japanese-inspired options.

3. Pure Cafe: Pure Cafe is a vegan-friendly cafe with multiple branches in Tokyo, including one in Aoyama. They serve a variety of vegan dishes, salads, wraps, smoothies, and desserts. The menu is focused on healthy and organic ingredients.

4. Brown Rice by Neal's Yard Remedies: Located in Omotesando, Brown Rice is a vegan-friendly restaurant that emphasizes organic, natural, and whole foods. They offer a variety of vegan dishes, including curries, grain bowls, and desserts.

5. Sora No Iro: Sora No Iro is a vegan restaurant located in Shibuya. They specialize in vegan Japanese cuisine, offering dishes like tempura, sushi, and noodle bowls, all made with plant-based ingredients.

6. Veganic To Go: Veganic To Go is a vegan fast-food restaurant with locations in various areas of Tokyo, such as Harajuku and Shimokitazawa. They offer vegan burgers, sandwiches, fries, and other quick bites.

7. Rainbow Raw Food: Located in Shinjuku, Rainbow Raw Food is a vegan restaurant that focuses on raw and organic cuisine. They serve a variety of raw dishes, salads, smoothies, and desserts.

8. Falafel Brothers: Falafel Brothers is a vegetarian and vegan-friendly restaurant located in Harajuku. They specialize in Middle Eastern cuisine, serving delicious falafel wraps, hummus, and other Mediterranean-inspired dishes.

These are just a few examples of the vegetarian and vegan options available in Tokyo. Additionally, many restaurants in the city are becoming more accommodating to plant-based diets, so you can often find vegetarian and vegan choices even at non-vegetarian/vegan establishments. It's always a good idea to check the menu or ask the staff about the ingredients to ensure they meet your dietary preferences.

Exploring Shinjuku

, we will take you on a journey through Shinjuku, one of Tokyo's most vibrant and dynamic neighborhoods. From the serene Shinjuku Gyoen National Garden to the bustling Kabukicho entertainment district and the exciting shopping scene, Shinjuku offers a plethora of attractions for visitors to explore.

Shinjuku Gyoen National Garden:
Start your exploration of Shinjuku with a visit to the tranquil Shinjuku Gyoen National Garden. Spanning 144 acres, this expansive garden is a peaceful oasis in the heart of the bustling city. Take a leisurely stroll through beautifully landscaped gardens, featuring traditional Japanese, French formal, and English landscape designs. Admire the stunning cherry blossoms in spring or the vibrant autumn foliage in the fall. Shinjuku Gyoen is the perfect place to relax, have a picnic, or simply escape the urban chaos.

Kabukicho Entertainment District:
Venture into the lively Kabukicho district, Tokyo's renowned entertainment and nightlife hub. Experience the electric atmosphere as you wander through neon-lit streets filled with

vibrant bars, clubs, and restaurants. Kabukicho is also known for its captivating blend of traditional and modern entertainment, including karaoke bars, pachinko parlors, and host and hostess clubs. Embrace the energy and excitement of this district, but be sure to exercise caution and follow local guidelines for a safe and enjoyable experience.

Shopping in Shinjuku:
Shinjuku offers an unparalleled shopping experience, catering to all tastes and budgets. Here are some shopping highlights:

- Department Stores: Explore the iconic department stores of Shinjuku, such as Isetan, Takashimaya, and Odakyu, which offer a wide range of luxury brands, fashion boutiques, cosmetics, and gourmet food halls. These grand establishments provide a blend of local and international products, making them perfect for a luxurious shopping spree.

- Shinjuku Mylord: Located near the bustling Shinjuku Station, Shinjuku Mylord is a multi-story shopping complex known for its trendy fashion stores, accessories, and lifestyle shops. It's an ideal destination for fashion enthusiasts looking for the latest trends.

- Omoide Yokocho: Step back in time as you visit Omoide Yokocho, also known as "Memory Lane" or "Piss Alley." This narrow alleyway is lined with small, atmospheric eateries and izakayas, where you can sample local street food and experience the nostalgic charm of post-war Tokyo.

- Lumine: For a more contemporary shopping experience, head to Lumine, a trendy shopping complex connected to Shinjuku Station. Lumine houses a wide selection of fashion boutiques, lifestyle stores, and restaurants, offering the latest trends and unique finds.

- Bicqlo: Located within the Bic Camera electronics store, Bicqlo is a fusion of Bic

Camera and Uniqlo. This innovative concept store combines the latest electronic gadgets with Uniqlo's popular clothing items, providing a unique shopping experience that caters to tech-savvy fashion enthusiasts.

Shinjuku's diverse shopping scene ensures that every visitor can find something to suit their preferences, whether it's high-end luxury, trendy fashion, or unique local products. Take your time to explore the various shopping areas and indulge in some retail therapy.

As you explore Shinjuku, keep in mind that it's a bustling district with a wide range of attractions. Plan your visit accordingly, considering the time of day and specific areas you want to explore. Shinjuku is also a transportation hub, making it easy to access other parts of Tokyo and beyond. Take advantage of the efficient public transportation system, including the Shinjuku Station, which is one of the busiest railway stations in the world.

In addition to the main attractions mentioned above, Shinjuku offers a multitude of dining options, from traditional Japanese cuisine to international flavors. Explore the narrow streets and alleys to discover hidden gems, local izakayas, and cozy cafes. Don't forget to try the regional specialties and street food offerings that will tantalize your taste buds.

Shinjuku is also home to cultural and entertainment venues, such as the Tokyo Metropolitan Government Building with its panoramic observation decks, where you can enjoy breathtaking views of the city skyline. The area also boasts theaters, art galleries, and live music venues, offering a diverse range of cultural experiences.

Lastly, immerse yourself in the vibrant atmosphere of Shinjuku's street life. From the vibrant street performers in Shinjuku's Kabukicho to the bustling crowds in the shopping districts, there is always something happening in this lively neighborhood. Take your time to soak in the energy and capture the essence of Tokyo's dynamic capital.

Remember to plan your visit to Shinjuku based on your interests and preferences. Whether you want to experience the tranquility of Shinjuku Gyoen National Garden, dive into the excitement of Kabukicho, indulge in shopping sprees, or savor the local cuisine, Shinjuku offers an unforgettable experience for every traveler.

Be sure to check the opening hours of attractions, make reservations when necessary, and familiarize yourself with the local customs and etiquette. With careful planning and an adventurous spirit, your exploration of Shinjuku will be a memorable part of your Tokyo journey.

Discovering Shibuya

we will guide you through the vibrant and fashionable neighborhood of Shibuya. Known for its iconic Shibuya Crossing, historical landmarks, and trendy fashion scene, Shibuya is a must-visit destination for travelers seeking a taste of Tokyo's urban culture.

6.1. Shibuya Crossing and Hachiko Statue:
Begin your exploration of Shibuya at one of the world's busiest intersections, Shibuya Crossing. Experience the organized chaos as crowds of pedestrians navigate the crossing from multiple directions, creating a mesmerizing spectacle. Capture the moment from one of the surrounding buildings for a bird's-eye view of this iconic scene.

While at Shibuya Crossing, don't miss the opportunity to visit the famous Hachiko Statue. This bronze statue commemorates Hachiko, an Akita dog known for his unwavering loyalty to his owner. The statue has become a symbol of Shibuya and a popular meeting point for locals and tourists alike. Take a moment to learn about the heartwarming story behind Hachiko and pay tribute to his loyalty.

 Meiji Jingu Shrine:
Escape the bustling city streets and step into the tranquility of Meiji Jingu Shrine, a serene oasis in the heart of Shibuya. Dedicated to Emperor Meiji and Empress Shoken, this Shinto shrine is surrounded by a lush forest, offering a peaceful retreat from the urban landscape. Take a leisurely walk along the tree-lined paths and admire the traditional architecture and serene atmosphere. If you're lucky, you may even witness a traditional Shinto wedding ceremony taking place.

Trendy Fashion and Shopping in Shibuya:
Shibuya is a fashion hub, attracting trendsetters from all over the world. Explore the fashionable streets of Shibuya and discover a wide range of clothing boutiques, department stores, and

trendy shopping centers. Here are a few highlights:

- Shibuya 109: Known as "Ichimarukyu," Shibuya 109 is a legendary fashion building that houses multiple floors of trendy boutiques, showcasing the latest Japanese fashion trends. Explore the extensive selection of women's clothing, accessories, and cosmetics, and experience the vibrant energy of Tokyo's youth fashion culture.

- Center Street and Koen-dori: Wander through the bustling streets of Center Street and Koen-dori to find a mix of independent fashion boutiques, vintage stores, and unique shops. Discover cutting-edge street fashion, quirky accessories, and alternative fashion trends that define Shibuya's eclectic style.

- Shibuya Stream: Visit the modern shopping complex of Shibuya Stream, which offers a blend of shopping, dining, and entertainment options. Enjoy the latest fashion brands, explore the food market, and relax in the rooftop garden while enjoying panoramic views of Shibuya.

- Tokyu Hands and Loft: For those seeking unique and innovative products, Tokyu Hands and Loft are a haven. These multi-story stores offer a wide range of lifestyle goods, including stationery, home decor, beauty products, and gadgets, making them ideal for finding distinctive souvenirs or indulging in retail therapy.

Shibuya's fashion and shopping scene is ever-evolving, showcasing the latest trends and fostering a creative and vibrant atmosphere. Take your time to explore the various shopping areas, immerse yourself in the local fashion culture, and discover unique pieces that reflect Tokyo's distinct style.

As you navigate Shibuya, don't forget to explore the charming side streets and alleys, which are often filled with trendy cafes, quirky shops, and local eateries. Embrace the youthful energy and vibrant street life that make Shibuya a captivating destination for visitors.

Plan your visit

When planning your visit to Shibuya, here are some tips to make the most of your time in this dynamic neighborhood:

1. Timing: Shibuya is busiest during weekdays and weekends, particularly in the evenings when people gather at Shibuya Crossing. Consider visiting in the morning or during weekdays for a less crowded experience.

2. Start at Shibuya Station: Begin your exploration at Shibuya Station, one of Tokyo's major transportation hubs. Take a moment to familiarize yourself with the station layout and exit locations as it can be quite large and busy. Use the Hachiko Exit to easily find the Hachiko Statue.

3. Shibuya Crossing: Don't miss the opportunity to witness the famous Shibuya Crossing in

action. Head to the pedestrian scramble from the nearby Starbucks or the Shibuya Mark City building for an excellent vantage point to observe and capture the bustling scene.

4. Visit Meiji Jingu Shrine: Take a leisurely stroll from Shibuya Crossing to Meiji Jingu Shrine, located within walking distance. Enjoy the peaceful atmosphere, lush greenery, and serene beauty of the shrine grounds. Check the shrine's website for any special events or ceremonies taking place during your visit.

5. Explore Center Street and Koen-dori: Immerse yourself in the trendy fashion scene by exploring Center Street and Koen-dori. These bustling streets offer a mix of independent boutiques, vintage shops, and unique stores. Take your time to browse through the diverse fashion offerings and discover hidden gems.

6. Shibuya 109 and Shibuya Stream: If you're interested in the latest fashion trends, be sure to visit Shibuya 109 and Shibuya Stream. Shibuya

109 is a fashion landmark with multiple floors dedicated to women's clothing and accessories. Shibuya Stream, on the other hand, offers a modern shopping experience with a variety of brands, dining options, and a rooftop garden.

7. Indulge in Local Cuisine: Shibuya is home to numerous restaurants and eateries, offering a wide range of dining options. Try local favorites such as ramen, sushi, or yakiniku (grilled meat) at one of the many restaurants scattered throughout the neighborhood. Don't forget to explore the smaller side streets for hidden culinary gems.

8. Nightlife in Shibuya: Shibuya comes alive at night with its vibrant nightlife scene. Explore the various bars, clubs, and entertainment venues in the area if you're looking to experience Tokyo's energetic nightlife. Be mindful of the local customs and follow guidelines for a safe and enjoyable evening.

Remember to wear comfortable shoes as Shibuya involves a fair amount of walking. Keep an eye on your belongings and be mindful of the crowd in busy areas. Take breaks in cozy cafes or parks to relax and soak up the atmosphere.

With careful planning and an adventurous spirit, your exploration of Shibuya will be an exciting and memorable part of your Tokyo adventure. Enjoy the bustling streets, trendy fashion, and vibrant energy that define this iconic neighborhood.

Unveiling Asakusa

we invite you to explore Asakusa, a neighborhood steeped in history and tradition. From the iconic Sensō-ji Temple to the bustling Nakamise Shopping Street and the abundance of traditional crafts and souvenirs, Asakusa offers a glimpse into Tokyo's rich cultural heritage.

Sensō-ji Temple:
Begin your journey in Asakusa by visiting Sensō-ji Temple, one of Tokyo's most significant and oldest Buddhist temples. As you approach the temple grounds, you will be greeted by the majestic Kaminarimon Gate, adorned with a massive red lantern and a symbol of Asakusa. Walk along Nakamise Shopping Street, which leads to the temple, and immerse yourself in the lively atmosphere filled with shops selling traditional snacks, souvenirs, and crafts.

Upon entering Sensō-ji Temple, take a moment to admire the stunning architecture, intricate details, and serene surroundings. Explore the main hall, where you can make offerings, light incense, and experience the peaceful ambiance of the temple. Don't forget to visit the adjacent Asakusa Shrine, dedicated to the Shinto deities. Capture the beauty of the temple complex and take in the spiritual essence that permeates the area.

Nakamise Shopping Street:
Adjacent to Sensō-ji Temple lies Nakamise Shopping Street, a vibrant and bustling arcade that stretches for approximately 250 meters. This historic shopping street is lined with numerous shops selling traditional Japanese snacks, sweets, souvenirs, and crafts. Indulge in some retail therapy as you browse through an array of unique items, including traditional clothing (kimono and yukata), folding fans, traditional toys, and calligraphy supplies. Nakamise Shopping Street offers a wonderful opportunity to immerse yourself in traditional Japanese culture and bring home authentic souvenirs.

Traditional Crafts and Souvenirs:
Asakusa is renowned for its traditional crafts and unique souvenirs. Beyond Nakamise Shopping Street, the neighborhood is dotted with shops and galleries where you can explore and purchase traditional crafts, ranging from ceramics and lacquerware to textiles and woodwork. Visit the nearby Asakusa Culture and Tourism Center or Tokyo Skytree Town Solamachi, which houses a variety of shops specializing in traditional crafts and local products. Take the time to appreciate the skill and craftsmanship behind these traditional creations and find a special memento to remember your time in Asakusa.

In addition to shopping, Asakusa offers a wide selection of traditional Japanese cuisine. Sample local delicacies such as tempura, soba noodles, and monjayaki at the numerous restaurants and food stalls in the area. Don't forget to try ningyo-yaki or senbei, traditional Japanese sweets that are popular souvenirs.

Asakusa's charm lies not only in its historical landmarks but also in its preservation of traditional Japanese culture. Take the opportunity to participate in cultural experiences, such as attending a traditional tea ceremony or trying on a kimono for a unique photo opportunity. Several cultural centers and workshops in Asakusa offer these immersive experiences, allowing you to delve deeper into the traditions and customs of Japan.

As you explore Asakusa, be mindful of the temple grounds' sacredness and the local customs. Respectfully observe any rules or guidelines in place and take off your shoes when entering designated areas. Keep in mind that Asakusa can get crowded, especially on weekends and holidays, so consider visiting during weekdays or early mornings for a more peaceful experience.

By delving into Asakusa's historical and cultural offerings, you can gain a deeper appreciation for Tokyo's rich heritage. Take your time to explore the hidden corners of this neighborhood, interact with locals, and learn about the traditions that have shaped Asakusa into what it is today.

Immerse yourself in the spiritual ambiance of Sensō-ji Temple, experience the lively atmosphere of Nakamise Shopping Street, and discover the artistry behind traditional crafts and souvenirs. Asakusa offers a blend of history, tradition, and vibrant street life, providing a truly immersive cultural experience.

Remember to respect the customs and traditions of the temple and its surroundings. Dress modestly and be mindful of photography restrictions, particularly within the temple complex. Take the opportunity to interact with the friendly shop owners and artisans, who are often more than willing to share stories and insights about their crafts.

Before leaving Asakusa, indulge in the local cuisine at one of the traditional restaurants or try some street food delicacies. From savory snacks to sweet treats, Asakusa's culinary scene is sure to delight your taste buds and leave you with fond memories of the flavors of Tokyo.

Asakusa's charm lies in its ability to transport you back in time while simultaneously embracing the present. It offers a unique juxtaposition of old and new, tradition and innovation. Take the time to appreciate the delicate balance between history and modernity as you explore this captivating neighborhood.

Whether you are seeking cultural enrichment, shopping for unique souvenirs, or simply soaking in the atmosphere of Tokyo's traditional side, Asakusa is a destination that will leave a lasting impression. Allow yourself to be enchanted by its timeless charm and uncover the hidden gems that make Asakusa a must-visit destination for any traveler in Tokyo.

With an open mind and a sense of curiosity, your journey through Asakusa will be filled with memorable encounters and a deeper understanding of Japan's cultural heritage. Enjoy the magic of Asakusa and embrace the spirit of exploration as you continue your Tokyo adventure.

Ueno Park and Museums

we invite you to explore Ueno Park and its hidden gems. Ueno Park is a sprawling green oasis in the heart of Tokyo, known for its cultural institutions, natural beauty, and vibrant market. Let's delve into the treasures awaiting you in this captivating corner of the city.

Tokyo National Museum:
Embark on a cultural journey at the Tokyo National Museum, Japan's oldest and largest museum. Housing an extensive collection of art and artifacts, the museum offers a comprehensive overview of Japan's rich history and diverse cultural heritage. Marvel at the exquisite works of art, including ancient pottery, samurai armor, delicate textiles, and centuries-old paintings. The museum's exhibits are organized into different galleries, allowing you to explore Japanese art, archaeology, and Asian artifacts. Plan your visit ahead and

consider joining a guided tour to gain deeper insights into the museum's treasures.

Ueno Zoo and Shinobazu Pond:
Adjacent to Ueno Park, you'll find the Ueno Zoo, a popular destination for animal enthusiasts of all ages. The zoo houses a wide range of species, including giant pandas, elephants, tigers, and various bird species. Take a leisurely stroll through the zoo's well-designed enclosures and learn about the conservation efforts in place to protect these fascinating creatures.

After exploring the zoo, head to Shinobazu Pond, a serene body of water located within Ueno Park. Admire the picturesque scenery and rent a paddleboat to leisurely navigate the pond's tranquil waters. Shinobazu Pond is also known for its lotus flowers, which bloom beautifully during the summer months, creating a stunning sight for visitors.

Ameya-Yokocho Market:

Immerse yourself in the lively atmosphere of Ameya-Yokocho Market, a bustling street market located near Ueno Station. Originally a black market after World War II, the market has transformed into a vibrant shopping district where you can find a wide variety of goods at affordable prices. From clothing and accessories to fresh produce and street food, Ameya-Yokocho offers a unique shopping experience with a blend of local flavors and international influences. Stroll through the narrow alleys, interact with friendly vendors, and indulge in delicious street snacks as you explore this lively market.

While in Ueno Park, take the opportunity to enjoy the park's natural beauty by wandering through its lush green spaces, picturesque ponds, and cherry blossom trees. Ueno Park is especially stunning during the cherry blossom season when the park transforms into a sea of delicate pink petals, attracting visitors from all over the world.

Additionally, Ueno Park is home to several other notable attractions, including the Ueno Toshogu Shrine, the Shitamachi Museum, and the Ueno Royal Museum. These hidden gems offer unique insights into Tokyo's history, traditional crafts, and art scene.

As you navigate Ueno Park and its hidden gems, take advantage of the various amenities available, such as picnic areas, restrooms, and food stalls. Consider visiting during weekdays or mornings to avoid larger crowds and make the most of your experience.

Ueno Park and its surrounding attractions are a testament to Tokyo's cultural richness and natural beauty. Explore the museums, appreciate the wildlife, and immerse yourself in the vibrant market atmosphere. Allow yourself to be captivated by the hidden gems that await you in this multifaceted corner of Tokyo.

With curiosity and an open mind, your journey through Ueno Park and its cultural treasures will be filled with unforgettable experiences and a deeper appreciation for Japan's art, nature, and history. Enjoy the serenity of the park, the wonders of the museum, and the bustling energy of the market. Embrace the diversity of experiences that Ueno Park has to offer, from moments of reflection to moments of excitement.

Take your time to explore the Tokyo National Museum, immersing yourself in the rich cultural heritage of Japan. Admire the masterpieces, learn about the historical significance of each artifact, and gain a deeper understanding of Japan's art, history, and traditions.

Afterward, venture into Ueno Zoo and encounter fascinating animals from around the world. Observe their behavior, learn about their habitats, and appreciate the importance of wildlife conservation. Don't forget to visit Shinobazu Pond, where you can relax and connect with nature, finding solace in its peaceful ambiance.

As you make your way through Ueno Park, let the vibrant atmosphere of Ameya-Yokocho Market ignite your senses. Immerse yourself in the bustling crowd, sample local street food, and engage in friendly banter with the enthusiastic vendors. Discover unique items, bargain for the best prices, and bring home a piece of Ueno's vibrant energy.

While in Ueno Park, make sure to take breaks and find quiet spots to unwind and appreciate the park's natural beauty. Whether it's finding a peaceful bench under the shade of a cherry blossom tree or enjoying a picnic by the pond, allow yourself to absorb the serenity and tranquility that the park offers.

Take advantage of the various amenities available, such as guided tours, information centers, and cultural events that may be happening during your visit. Check the park's schedule for any special exhibitions, performances, or festivals that you can attend to enhance your experience.

Remember to respect the surroundings, follow any rules or guidelines, and be mindful of the environment. Ueno Park is a cherished space for locals and visitors alike, and by showing respect, you contribute to the preservation of its natural and cultural heritage.

As you uncover the hidden gems of Ueno Park, let your curiosity guide you and embrace the blend of nature, culture, and excitement that awaits. Allow yourself to be captivated by the serenity of the park, the knowledge within the museums, and the lively atmosphere of the market. Ueno Park is a true gem within Tokyo, offering a diverse range of experiences that will leave a lasting impression.

Enjoy your journey through Ueno Park and its hidden treasures, and may it inspire you to further explore the beauty and wonders of Tokyo's dynamic capital.

Odaiba: Tokyo's Futuristic Island

we will explore Odaiba, a futuristic island that showcases Tokyo's modernity and technological advancements. From entertainment complexes to stunning waterfront views, Odaiba offers a unique and immersive experience in the heart of the city.

 Palette Town and Mega Web:
Kick off your Odaiba adventure at Palette Town, a vibrant complex filled with entertainment options. Visit Mega Web, an automotive theme park where you can explore the world of cars and experience virtual driving simulators. Marvel at the displays of futuristic vehicles and get a glimpse into the future of transportation. Don't forget to take a ride on the Giant Sky Wheel for panoramic views of Tokyo Bay and the surrounding cityscape.

Odaiba Seaside Park and Beaches:
Take a leisurely stroll along Odaiba Seaside Park, a waterfront promenade offering stunning views of Tokyo Bay. Enjoy the sea breeze and take in the sights of Rainbow Bridge and the Tokyo skyline. If you visit during the summer months, you can relax on one of Odaiba's man-made beaches, such as Odaiba Beach Park or Kasai Rinkai Park. These beaches provide a refreshing escape from the bustling city and are perfect for sunbathing, picnicking, or simply enjoying the waterfront ambiance.

TeamLab Borderless Exhibition:
Immerse yourself in a world of digital art at the TeamLab Borderless Exhibition in Odaiba. This interactive and immersive art installation showcases the intersection of art and technology through mesmerizing light displays, projections, and sensor-activated artworks. Lose yourself in the stunning visual landscapes and let your senses be captivated by the ever-changing environments. This unique exhibition offers a

truly unforgettable experience that combines art, technology, and creativity.

While in Odaiba, take the opportunity to explore other attractions in the area, such as the futuristic shopping malls of Aqua City and VenusFort, which offer a wide range of shops, restaurants, and entertainment options. Visit the Odaiba Statue of Liberty, a replica of the iconic statue, and capture memorable photos against the backdrop of Tokyo Bay.

To reach Odaiba, you can take the Yurikamome Line, a driverless train that offers panoramic views as it crosses the Rainbow Bridge. Alternatively, you can access the island via the Tokyo Water Bus, which provides a scenic journey along the Sumida River.

As you explore Odaiba, make sure to check the schedules and availability of attractions and exhibitions in advance. Some experiences may require timed entry tickets, so it's advisable to plan accordingly. Also, take note of the sunset time, as Odaiba's waterfront offers stunning views during twilight and into the evening.

Odaiba's futuristic ambiance, stunning waterfront views, and technological marvels make it a must-visit destination for travelers seeking a unique experience in Tokyo. Whether you're a technology enthusiast, an art lover, or simply looking to unwind by the beach, Odaiba has something for everyone.

Enjoy your journey through Odaiba's Palette Town, Mega Web, Odaiba Seaside Park, and the mesmerizing TeamLab Borderless Exhibition. Immerse yourself in the modernity and innovation that Tokyo's futuristic island has to offer, and create memories that will last a lifetime.

Exploring Old Tokyo: Yanaka and Nezu

we will delve into the charm and rich history of Old Tokyo, specifically the neighborhoods of Yanaka and Nezu. These areas offer a glimpse into the traditional side of the city, with their preserved architecture, serene shrines, and cultural workshops.

Yanaka Ginza Shopping Street:
Begin your exploration of Yanaka by strolling along Yanaka Ginza Shopping Street, a charming retro-style street lined with small shops and local vendors. This lively street offers a wide variety of goods, including traditional snacks, handicrafts, clothing, and souvenirs. Immerse yourself in the nostalgic atmosphere as you wander through the bustling crowds, and take the opportunity to sample local street food such as taiyaki (fish-shaped cakes) or dango (sweet rice dumplings). Yanaka Ginza Shopping Street is a perfect place to experience the

authentic local culture and interact with friendly shopkeepers.

Nezu Shrine and Yanaka Cemetery:
Visit the picturesque Nezu Shrine, a hidden gem nestled in the heart of Yanaka. This Shinto shrine is known for its vermilion torii gates, beautiful gardens, and traditional architecture. Take a moment to explore the tranquil grounds, wander through the winding paths, and admire the vibrant colors of the azalea flowers during the spring season. Nezu Shrine provides a serene escape from the bustling city and offers a glimpse into Japan's ancient spiritual traditions.

Adjacent to Nezu Shrine is the Yanaka Cemetery, a historic cemetery known for its peaceful ambiance and beautifully maintained grounds. Take a contemplative walk through the pathways, surrounded by towering trees and moss-covered tombstones. Yanaka Cemetery is not only a place of final rest but also a testament to Tokyo's history and the lives of the people who shaped the city.

Traditional Arts and Crafts Workshops:
Yanaka and Nezu are home to several traditional arts and crafts workshops, where you can engage in hands-on experiences and learn about traditional Japanese craftsmanship. Join a pottery or ceramics class, try your hand at calligraphy, or participate in a traditional tea ceremony. These workshops offer a unique opportunity to gain insights into Japan's rich artistic heritage and create your own piece of traditional art under the guidance of skilled artisans.

In addition to the main attractions mentioned above, take the time to wander through the narrow streets of Yanaka and Nezu, where you can discover old temples, preserved wooden houses, and small local museums. Embrace the nostalgic atmosphere, interact with the friendly residents, and uncover the hidden gems that these neighborhoods have to offer.

While exploring Yanaka and Nezu, keep in mind the importance of respecting the local customs and traditions. Dress modestly when visiting shrines and temples, and be mindful of any photography restrictions. Engage with the locals respectfully, and perhaps even take the opportunity to learn a few basic Japanese phrases to enhance your interactions.

Old Tokyo's Yanaka and Nezu neighborhoods offer a peaceful and authentic experience, allowing you to step back in time and connect with the city's traditional roots. Enjoy the lively atmosphere of Yanaka Ginza Shopping Street, find solace in the tranquility of Nezu Shrine and Yanaka Cemetery, and embrace the opportunity to participate in traditional arts and crafts workshops. Through these experiences, you will gain a deeper appreciation for Tokyo's cultural heritage and the craftsmanship that has been passed down through generations.

Take your time to explore the hidden corners of Yanaka and Nezu, and allow yourself to be captivated by the nostalgic charm and rich history that permeate these neighborhoods. Enjoy the old-world ambiance, connect with local residents, and create lasting memories of your journey through Old Tokyo. Immerse yourself in the traditions, crafts, and spirituality that define Yanaka and Nezu, and appreciate the beauty of a Tokyo that existed long before the city's modern transformation.

As you explore Yanaka Ginza Shopping Street, engage in conversations with the shopkeepers and vendors, and learn about their stories and the history of the neighborhood. Embrace the warm hospitality and friendly atmosphere, and perhaps even try your hand at traditional Japanese games or indulge in some local delicacies.

When visiting Nezu Shrine, take a moment to offer a prayer or pay your respects. Take in the tranquility of the surroundings, listen to the soothing sounds of nature, and appreciate the architectural details that reflect the craftsmanship of bygone eras. Capture the essence of spiritual serenity and reflect on the significance of the shrine in Japanese culture.

In Yanaka Cemetery, walk in quiet contemplation among the tombstones and pay homage to the individuals who have left their mark on Tokyo's history. Respect the solemnity of the space and take a moment to appreciate the beauty of the carefully manicured landscapes, which provide a peaceful retreat from the busy city.

Participating in traditional arts and crafts workshops allows you to not only witness but also engage in the artistic traditions of Japan. Learn from skilled artisans who are passionate about preserving these crafts and pass on their knowledge to visitors. Embrace the opportunity to create your own unique piece of art and take home a tangible reminder of your experience in Old Tokyo.

While exploring Yanaka and Nezu, take the time to observe and appreciate the everyday life of the locals. Observe the architectural details of the traditional houses, notice the small shrines tucked away in corners, and allow yourself to be captivated by the simple beauty that lies within these historic neighborhoods.

As you navigate the streets of Old Tokyo, remember to be respectful of the residents and their privacy. Avoid making excessive noise and refrain from littering. Embrace the spirit of curiosity and open-mindedness, and be open to learning and experiencing new aspects of Japanese culture.

By immersing yourself in the old-world ambiance of Yanaka and Nezu, you will gain a deeper understanding of Tokyo's cultural heritage and the traditions that continue to shape the city. Take the time to appreciate the stories embedded in these neighborhoods, and let the authenticity and charm of Old Tokyo leave a lasting impression on your journey.

Embrace the opportunity to connect with local residents, listen to their stories, and engage in meaningful interactions. Through these encounters, you will gain insights into the daily life of Tokyoites and foster a deeper appreciation for the city's rich cultural tapestry.

As you bid farewell to Yanaka and Nezu, carry with you the memories of the old-world ambiance, the warmth of the local residents, and the artistic expressions that define this unique part of Tokyo. Allow the experiences in Old Tokyo to enrich your understanding of the city's past and present, and inspire you to continue exploring the diverse facets of Japan's dynamic capital.

Tokyo's Temples and Shrines

we will explore Tokyo's temples and shrines, which offer a glimpse into the city's spiritual and cultural heritage. These sacred sites provide a serene escape from the bustling city and offer an opportunity for reflection and connection with Japan's rich traditions.

Meiji Shrine:
Located in the heart of Tokyo, Meiji Shrine is a symbol of Japan's spiritual and historical significance. Dedicated to Emperor Meiji and Empress Shoken, this Shinto shrine is nestled within a peaceful forest, creating an oasis of tranquility in the bustling city. As you approach the shrine, you'll pass through towering torii gates and walk along a path lined with majestic trees. Take the time to cleanse your hands and mouth at the chozuya (water pavilion) before entering the main shrine area. Explore the spacious grounds, visit the Inner Garden, and

perhaps even witness a traditional wedding ceremony. Meiji Shrine offers a serene and immersive experience that allows you to connect with Japan's imperial past and the enduring legacy of Emperor Meiji.

Senso-ji Temple:
Located in Asakusa, Senso-ji Temple is one of Tokyo's oldest and most significant Buddhist temples. As you approach the temple, you'll pass through the iconic Kaminarimon Gate, adorned with a large red lantern and two imposing statues. Stroll along Nakamise Shopping Street, lined with shops selling traditional snacks, souvenirs, and crafts, before reaching the main temple area. Take in the intricate details of the temple's architecture, and if you're fortunate, witness a Buddhist ceremony or participate in a prayer ritual. Explore the temple's various halls and pagodas, and ascend to the observation deck for a panoramic view of Asakusa and the Tokyo skyline. Senso-ji Temple is not only a place of worship but also a cultural hub, offering a

glimpse into the rich traditions of Buddhism and Japanese craftsmanship.

Hie Shrine and Zozoji Temple:
Located near Tokyo Tower, Hie Shrine is known for its picturesque setting and vibrant festivals. This Shinto shrine offers a peaceful retreat from the surrounding urban landscape, with its beautiful garden and lush greenery. Take a moment to admire the main shrine building, which features a distinct red color and intricate architectural details. Hie Shrine is particularly popular during the Setsubun Festival in February, when visitors participate in bean-throwing ceremonies to ward off evil spirits and bring good fortune for the year ahead.

Zozoji Temple, situated adjacent to Tokyo Tower, is a significant Buddhist temple that dates back to the 14th century. Explore the temple's expansive grounds, which house various structures, including a massive wooden gate and a mausoleum dedicated to the Tokugawa family. As you wander through the temple complex, take note of the beautifully manicured gardens and the serene atmosphere that permeates the area. Zozoji Temple holds cultural and religious importance and is a place where visitors can gain insights into the history and spirituality of Japan.

While visiting these temples and shrines, it's important to be respectful of the sacred nature of the sites. Dress modestly, observe any photography restrictions, and follow proper etiquette when participating in rituals or ceremonies. Engage with the local customs, such as purifying yourself with water before entering the shrine or temple, and show reverence for the traditions and beliefs of the Japanese people.

Tokyo's temples and shrines provide an opportunity to delve deeper into the spiritual and cultural fabric of the city. Whether you seek inner peace, a connection to Japan's history, or simply a moment of reflection and tranquility, Tokyo's temples and shrines offer a serene and introspective experience. These sacred sites allow you to step away from the fast-paced urban environment and immerse yourself in the rich cultural and spiritual heritage of Japan.

As you visit Meiji Shrine, Senso-ji Temple, Hie Shrine, and Zozoji Temple, take the time to appreciate the beauty and craftsmanship of the architecture. Notice the intricate details, the vibrant colors, and the sense of serenity that envelops these sacred spaces. Allow yourself to be in the present moment, letting the peaceful atmosphere wash over you and inviting a sense of calm and introspection.

Engage with the rituals and customs of each temple and shrine, such as offering a prayer, lighting incense, or making a wish. Respectfully observe the practices of other visitors and follow the guidance of the temple or shrine staff. Take part in the activities that resonate with you, whether it's writing a wish on an ema (prayer plaque), spinning the prayer wheels, or participating in a guided meditation session.

Beyond the religious significance, these temples and shrines are also cultural landmarks that offer a window into Japan's history and traditions. Take the opportunity to learn about the stories and legends associated with each site, as well as the historical context in which they were established. Engage with the information boards, attend guided tours if available, or consider hiring a knowledgeable local guide to gain deeper insights into the significance of these places.

Tokyo's temples and shrines are often surrounded by beautiful gardens or other points of interest. Take the time to explore the surrounding areas, such as Meiji Shrine's Inner Garden, which offers a serene and scenic escape from the city, or the Nakamise Shopping Street leading to Senso-ji Temple, where you can find unique souvenirs and traditional snacks. These additional attractions add to the overall experience and provide a well-rounded visit to each location.

While exploring Tokyo's temples and shrines, remember to maintain a respectful demeanor. Keep noise levels to a minimum, avoid touching or damaging any sacred objects or structures, and adhere to any specific rules or guidelines provided by the staff. Remember that these sites hold deep spiritual and cultural significance to the local community, and it is important to honor and preserve their sanctity.

Whether you are seeking a moment of tranquility, a deeper connection to Japanese history and spirituality, or simply a chance to reflect and find inner peace, Tokyo's temples and shrines offer a respite from the bustling city and a gateway to a world of cultural richness and contemplation. Allow yourself to be present in the moment, embrace the spiritual ambiance, and let the profound serenity of these sacred sites leave a lasting impression on your journey through Tokyo.

Gardens and Parks in Tokyo

we will explore Tokyo's exquisite gardens and parks, where you can escape the urban hustle and bustle and immerse yourself in nature's beauty. These carefully curated green spaces offer a serene retreat, providing a perfect balance to the vibrant energy of the city. Let's discover the tranquility and natural wonders of Rikugien Garden, Hamarikyu Gardens, and Shinjuku Gyoen National Garden.

Rikugien Garden:
Located in the Bunkyo ward, Rikugien Garden is a masterpiece of traditional Japanese landscaping. Designed during the Edo period, this garden is known for its breathtaking scenery that changes with the seasons. As you stroll along the winding paths, you'll encounter meticulously manicured lawns, tranquil ponds, and meticulously placed rocks and trees. Take a moment to admire the iconic Tsutsuji-ya (Azalea Hill) during the spring bloom or marvel at the

vibrant autumn foliage reflected in the garden's pond. Rikugien Garden offers a serene atmosphere, inviting you to relax and appreciate the harmony between man-made beauty and the natural world.

Hamarikyu Gardens:
Situated near Tokyo Bay in the Chuo ward, Hamarikyu Gardens is a picturesque landscape that seamlessly blends traditional Japanese gardening techniques with the surrounding waterfront views. This garden boasts a teahouse on a small island, where you can experience a traditional tea ceremony while overlooking a tranquil pond. Explore the various themed gardens, including the pine tree-lined pathway and the vibrant flower beds. During the autumn season, witness the stunning transformation of the garden as the trees turn vibrant shades of red and gold. Hamarikyu Gardens is an oasis of calm in the heart of the city, offering a chance to reconnect with nature and appreciate the meticulous artistry of Japanese garden design.

Shinjuku Gyoen National Garden:
Covering a vast area in Shinjuku, Shinjuku Gyoen National Garden is a popular destination for locals and visitors alike. This expansive park features a harmonious blend of traditional Japanese, French formal, and English landscape styles. Explore the meticulously maintained lawns, meandering walking paths, and serene ponds. With over 20,000 trees from various species, Shinjuku Gyoen National Garden offers a stunning display of cherry blossoms during the spring season, creating a breathtaking sea of pink. The garden also provides a peaceful retreat during the autumn months when the foliage transforms into a vibrant tapestry of red, orange, and yellow. Take a break at one of the park's tea houses and savor the tranquility that surrounds you.

When visiting Tokyo's gardens and parks, take your time to fully appreciate the natural beauty and serenity they offer. Slow down your pace, find a quiet spot to sit and contemplate, or enjoy a leisurely picnic amidst the lush greenery.

Engage your senses by listening to the gentle sounds of flowing water, inhaling the fragrance of blooming flowers, and observing the delicate movements of wildlife.

Remember to respect the rules and guidelines of each garden or park, such as refraining from stepping on restricted areas, not littering, and adhering to any photography regulations. Be mindful of the peace and quiet that others seek in these spaces, and maintain a respectful distance from any wildlife you may encounter.

Tokyo's gardens and parks are not only places of natural beauty but also cultural treasures that reflect the deep appreciation of harmony and aesthetics in Japanese culture. They offer an escape from the urban jungle and provide an opportunity to connect with the tranquility and serenity of nature. Whether you seek a moment of solitude, a peaceful walk, or a vibrant display of seasonal colors, Rikugien Garden, Hamarikyu Gardens, and Shinjuku Gyoen National Garden have something unique to offer. Each garden has its own charm and distinct features that make it worth exploring.

Rikugien Garden is renowned for its meticulous design and breathtaking landscapes. As you wander through the garden, you'll encounter stunning vistas, serene tea houses, and picturesque bridges. The garden's name, which means "six poems garden," reflects its poetic beauty and the inspiration it provides to visitors. Whether you visit during the cherry blossom season, when the garden is adorned with delicate pink blooms, or in the autumn, when the maple trees turn into a fiery spectacle, Rikugien Garden offers a serene and enchanting experience.

Hamarikyu Gardens, with its unique blend of traditional Japanese and waterfront views, offers a tranquil escape in the heart of the city. The garden's teahouse on a small island is a must-visit spot where you can partake in a traditional tea ceremony while surrounded by the garden's natural splendor. Take a leisurely stroll along the garden's paths, admire the meticulously pruned pine trees, and enjoy the contrasting landscapes of the pond and the Tokyo Bay skyline. Hamarikyu Gardens is a perfect place to find solace and reconnect with nature.

Shinjuku Gyoen National Garden, one of Tokyo's largest parks, is a haven of greenery and natural beauty. With its expansive lawns, colorful flower beds, and diverse range of trees, the park offers a delightful escape from the city's hustle and bustle. Whether you want to take a leisurely walk, have a picnic, or simply sit and enjoy the serenity, Shinjuku Gyoen National Garden has plenty of space for you to unwind. The garden's cherry blossoms in spring and vibrant autumn foliage create stunning seasonal displays that attract visitors from around the world.

As you explore these gardens, be sure to take your time, breathe in the fresh air, and let the beauty of nature soothe your senses. Pause at scenic viewpoints, find a quiet bench to sit on, or participate in a guided tour to learn more about the history and significance of each garden. Carry a camera to capture the picturesque landscapes and create lasting memories of your visit.

Whether you're a nature enthusiast, a photography lover, or someone seeking a peaceful escape, Rikugien Garden, Hamarikyu Gardens, and Shinjuku Gyoen National Garden offer a rejuvenating experience in the heart of Tokyo. Let the beauty of these gardens inspire and uplift you as you immerse yourself in the tranquility of nature.

Tokyo by Night

After the sun sets, Tokyo transforms into a vibrant and dynamic city that comes alive with a pulsating nightlife. In this chapter, we will explore some of the most exciting and captivating nighttime experiences Tokyo has to offer. Get ready to immerse yourself in the energetic atmosphere of Roppongi, uncover the historic charm of Golden Gai, and venture into the bustling alleyways of Omoide Yokocho in Shinjuku.

Nightlife in Roppongi:
Roppongi is renowned for its lively nightlife scene, with a plethora of bars, clubs, and entertainment venues to suit all tastes. This district caters to both locals and international visitors, offering a diverse range of experiences. From upscale clubs with renowned DJs to cozy jazz bars and trendy cocktail lounges, Roppongi

has it all. Indulge in delicious cuisine at the area's many restaurants before stepping into the vibrant nightclubs to dance the night away. Roppongi is the perfect destination for those seeking an electrifying and cosmopolitan nightlife experience.

Golden Gai: Tokyo's Historic Bar District:
Step back in time and experience the nostalgic charm of Golden Gai, a historic bar district in Shinjuku. This maze of narrow alleyways is lined with tiny bars, each with its unique theme and atmosphere. Despite its small size, Golden Gai is a hub for artists, musicians, and locals looking for an intimate and cozy drinking experience. Explore the diverse range of bars, from jazz and rock-themed establishments to bars specializing in craft cocktails or showcasing traditional Japanese culture. Engage in conversations with the friendly bartenders and fellow patrons, immersing yourself in the rich tapestry of Golden Gai's vibrant nightlife.

Omoide Yokocho: The Pulsating Alleyways of Shinjuku:

Located near Shinjuku Station, Omoide Yokocho (Memory Lane), also known as "Piss Alley," is a fascinating and bustling maze of narrow alleyways filled with tiny eateries and bars. This atmospheric enclave is reminiscent of old Tokyo, offering a glimpse into the city's post-war era. As you wander through the labyrinthine alleyways, you'll be captivated by the tantalizing aromas of sizzling yakitori (grilled skewered chicken) and other mouthwatering street food. Pull up a stool at a cozy izakaya (Japanese pub), order a drink, and savor the vibrant atmosphere as locals and visitors alike gather to enjoy the lively ambiance of this unique culinary and social hub.

When exploring Tokyo's nightlife, it's important to keep in mind some considerations. Take note of the dress codes and age restrictions at certain venues, as some establishments may have specific policies. It's also advisable to keep an eye on your belongings and exercise caution, as popular nightlife areas can sometimes get crowded. Respect the local customs and be mindful of noise levels and behavior to ensure a positive and enjoyable experience for yourself and others.

Whether you're in the mood for a glamorous night out in Roppongi, a nostalgic adventure in Golden Gai, or a vibrant culinary exploration in Omoide Yokocho, Tokyo's nighttime offerings promise excitement, diversity, and unforgettable memories. Embrace the energy, immerse yourself in the pulsating atmosphere, and discover the captivating allure of Tokyo after dark.

Tokyo hidden gem

Tokyo, the bustling capital of Japan, is filled with amazing attractions and hidden gems that may not be as well-known to tourists. Here are some hidden gems in Tokyo worth exploring:

1. Yanaka Ginza: This charming shopping street in the Yanaka neighborhood retains a nostalgic atmosphere with its traditional shops, street food stalls, and small cafes. It's a great place to experience a more relaxed and traditional side of Tokyo.

2. Kagurazaka: Located near the Iidabashi station, Kagurazaka is a historic neighborhood with narrow streets, traditional buildings, and a mix of French and Japanese influences. Explore the winding alleys, visit the traditional shops, and enjoy the numerous restaurants serving delicious French and Japanese cuisine.

3. Shimokitazawa: Known for its alternative and bohemian vibe, Shimokitazawa is a hip neighborhood filled with vintage clothing stores, quirky shops, and small theaters. It's a great place to find unique fashion items, vinyl records, and enjoy live music performances.

4. Gado-shita (under the train tracks) in Yurakucho: Yurakucho's Gado-shita area is

tucked beneath the train tracks and is a hidden culinary hotspot. You'll find numerous small izakayas (Japanese pubs) and restaurants serving a variety of mouthwatering dishes. It's a popular spot for locals to enjoy after-work drinks and delicious food.

5. Todoroki Valley: Escape the hustle and bustle of the city and find tranquility in Todoroki Valley. Located in Setagaya, this hidden gem features a lush green valley with a small river, a stone bridge, and a walking path lined with cherry trees. It's a beautiful place to take a leisurely stroll and enjoy nature.

6. Nakano Broadway: While Akihabara gets much of the attention for anime and manga, Nakano Broadway offers a more authentic and less crowded experience. This shopping complex is packed with stores selling anime merchandise, collectibles, retro video games, and manga. It's a paradise for enthusiasts of Japanese pop culture.

7. Omoide Yokocho: Situated near Shinjuku Station, Omoide Yokocho (Memory Lane) is a narrow alleyway lined with tiny traditional izakayas. The nostalgic atmosphere, delicious street food, and the wafting smell of yakitori (grilled chicken skewers) make it a must-visit spot for food lovers.

8. Koishikawa Korakuen Garden: This stunning traditional Japanese garden is often overlooked by visitors. Located near Tokyo Dome, it features meticulously landscaped gardens, ponds, teahouses, and walking paths. It's a serene oasis in the heart of the city, especially beautiful during cherry blossom season.

Remember, Tokyo is a city full of surprises, and these are just a few hidden gems among many. Exploring the lesser-known areas can provide a more intimate and authentic experience of the city's culture and lifestyle.

Things I found interest on my visit to Tokyo

It's great to hear about the interesting things you found during your visit to Tokyo! Here's some additional information about the points you mentioned:

1. Clean Roads and Limited Bins: Tokyo is known for its cleanliness, and you're right that the streets are generally kept very clean. However, it's true that you may notice a relative scarcity of public trash bins compared to other cities. This is because the Japanese emphasis is on personal responsibility for disposing of garbage properly. It's common for people to carry their trash with them until they find a suitable place to dispose of it.

2. High-Tech Restrooms: Japan is renowned for its advanced toilet technology. Many public restrooms in Tokyo are equipped with high-tech features such as heated seats, bidet functions, adjustable water pressure, air dryers, and even sound effects to mask any sounds you might make. These innovative restrooms provide a unique and comfortable experience.

3. Rice in Japanese Cuisine: Rice is a staple food in Japan, and it is indeed a significant part of Japanese cuisine. It's commonly served with various dishes, including sushi, sashimi, curry, and traditional Japanese

meals. Trying a rice burger is a great way to experience a fusion of Western and Japanese flavors.

4. Quiet Trains: The trains in Tokyo are known for their punctuality and efficiency. One noticeable aspect is the quiet atmosphere on board. Passengers generally maintain a respectful silence during their commutes, which contributes to a peaceful and calm environment, especially during rush hours.

Thank you for sharing your experiences, and I hope you had a memorable time exploring Tokyo!

FAQs

What is the cost of a flight from the United States to Tokyo?

Depending on the airline, the season, and how far in advance you book, a ticket to Tokyo from the United States might cost different amounts. A round-trip ticket typically costs between $600 and $1,200.

What is the typical price of a hotel room in Tokyo?

Depending on the type of lodging, the area, and the season, the cost of lodging in Tokyo can change. A mid-range hotel may cost between $100 and $200 per night, whereas a budget hotel may cost between $50 and $100 per night. The average nightly rate for a luxury hotel is $300 or more.

How much should I set aside for meals and beverages in Tokyo?

Where you go and what you eat might affect the price of food and drink in Tokyo. A lunch at a mid-range restaurant can cost between $20 and $40 per person on average, whereas a meal at a budget restaurant can cost between $10 and $15 per person. In Tokyo, alcoholic beverages may be rather pricey, with a beer going for anywhere from $5 to $8.

Are there any attractions in Tokyo that are free?

Yes, there are many free things to do in Tokyo. These include going to parks and gardens like Yoyogi Park or Shinjuku Gyoen, discovering the historical Asakusa neighborhood or the cutting-edge buildings of Omotesando, and even going to some museums like the Tokyo Metropolitan Government Building Observatory or the Imperial Palace East Gardens.

Does my trip to Tokyo require me to buy travel insurance?

Although travel insurance is not required when visiting Tokyo, it is strongly advised to obtain it to protect yourself from unanticipated events like medical emergencies, trip cancellations, or lost luggage. Depending on the extent of coverage and length of your trip, the cost of travel insurance can range from $50 to $150.

Advice on How to Save Money in Tokyo

Although Tokyo is seen as a vibrant, fascinating city, it can also be rather pricey. However, with enough preparation and insider knowledge, it's feasible to cut costs while still taking advantage of all that Tokyo has to offer. Here are some suggestions for budgeting in Tokyo:

1. Take the bus or train

As was previously established, Tokyo boasts a robust public transit system. Not only is taking public transportation economical, but it's also a terrific way to see a city like a resident.

2. Consume locally.

Saving money on food expenses can be accomplished by eating like a local. Take into account experimenting with inexpensive options like ramen, sushi, and fast food.

3. Check out free sights to see

Parks and temples are just a few of Tokyo's many free attractions. Not only are these sites reasonably priced, but visiting them is a wonderful way to get a taste of the local way of life.

4. Visit thrift shops

Tokyo offers many secondhand shops and flea markets where you can find unusual products for a small fraction of the price of new ones.

Conclusion: Tokyo Unveiled

Congratulations! You have embarked on a journey through the dynamic capital of Japan, Tokyo. From the bustling streets of Shinjuku and Shibuya to the serene gardens of Rikugien and Shinjuku Gyoen, you have explored the diverse facets of this incredible city. Along the way, you have discovered the rich cultural heritage, indulged in mouthwatering cuisine, and experienced the vibrant nightlife that Tokyo has to offer.

As your Tokyo adventure comes to a close, it's important to keep a few travel tips and resources in mind to ensure a smooth and memorable trip. Let's delve into some essential information to help you navigate the city like a pro.

 Language Tips and Useful Phrases:
While English is widely spoken in tourist areas, it's always helpful to know a few basic Japanese phrases to enhance your interactions and show

respect for the local culture. Simple greetings like "Konnichiwa" (Hello) and "Arigatou gozaimasu" (Thank you) go a long way in establishing a friendly connection. Familiarize yourself with common phrases related to transportation, ordering food, and asking for directions. This will not only make your experience more enjoyable but also demonstrate your appreciation for the local language and customs.

Shopping and Souvenir Guide:
Tokyo is a shopping paradise, offering a wide range of shopping options catering to different tastes and budgets. From luxury department stores in Ginza to trendy fashion boutiques in Shibuya, you'll find everything from high-end designer brands to unique, locally made goods. Take advantage of tax-free shopping for tourists by carrying your passport and look out for specialty stores that offer traditional crafts, tea, and other unique Japanese souvenirs. Don't forget to explore bustling markets like

Ameya-Yokocho and Nakamise Shopping Street for a vibrant and authentic shopping experience.

Recommended App

Online resources such as official tourism websites and travel blogs offer up-to-date information on events, festivals, and local recommendations. Additionally,

Certainly! Here are some smartphone apps that can be useful during your visit to Tokyo:

1. Google Maps: Google Maps is a versatile app that provides navigation, real-time traffic updates, public transportation information, and walking directions. It can help you navigate Tokyo's extensive train and subway system, find nearby attractions, restaurants, and other points of interest.

2. Tokyo Metro: The official Tokyo Metro app is specifically designed for navigating the subway system in Tokyo. It provides route planning, fare information, station maps, and real-time train schedules. It can be particularly helpful for

navigating the complex network of subway lines in the city.

3. Japan Travel: The Japan Travel app is a comprehensive resource for travelers in Japan. It offers information on popular tourist destinations, local attractions, events, accommodations, and dining options. It also provides travel guides and helpful tips for exploring Tokyo and other parts of Japan.

4. Google Translator: The Google Translate app is a valuable tool for overcoming language barriers during your visit to Tokyo. It can translate text, images, and even spoken words. You can use it to translate signs, menus, and have basic conversations with locals. It supports offline translation as well, which can be useful if you don't have a data connection.

These apps can greatly enhance your experience in Tokyo by providing navigation assistance, travel information, and language translation. Remember to download them before your trip and have a reliable internet connection or data plan to make the most out of their features.

are invaluable tools for navigating the city, finding transportation routes, and discovering nearby attractions.

As you bid farewell to Tokyo, take a moment to reflect on the incredible experiences and memories you have created during your time in this captivating city. Tokyo's vibrant energy, rich cultural heritage, and warm hospitality will stay with you long after you leave. Remember to embrace the Japanese customs, be respectful towards the local traditions, and immerse yourself in the unique blend of old-world charm and futuristic innovation that Tokyo embodies.

Whether you return to Tokyo in the future or embark on new adventures elsewhere, the lessons learned and the memories made in this dynamic capital will forever enrich your travel experiences. Tokyo, with its captivating blend of tradition and modernity, will always welcome you back with open arms.

Arigatou gozaimashita! (Thank you very much!) Safe travels and may your future journeys be filled with wonder and discovery!

Printed in Great Britain
by Amazon

24069715R00106